The Case for the Existence of God

by **Bert Thompson, Ph.D.**
and **Wayne Jackson, M.A.**

Apologetics Press, Inc.
230 Landmark Drive
Montgomery, Alabama 36117-2752

© Copyright 1996
ISBN: 0-932859-28-3
All rights reserved. No part of this book may be reproduced in any form without permission from the publisher, except in the case of brief quotations embodied in articles or critical reviews.

Other Titles In This Series
The Bible Translation Controversy
The Christian and Medical Ethics
Faith and Reason
The Global Flood of Noah
The Scientific Case for Creation

TABLE OF CONTENTS

CHAPTER ONE	Introduction 1	
CHAPTER TWO	Cause and Effect— The Cosmological Argument 3	
	Is the Universe Eternal?	5
	Did the Universe Create Itself Out of Nothing?	7
	Was the Universe Created?	10
CHAPTER THREE	Design in Nature— The Teleological Argument........ 15	
	Design of the Universe	18
	Design of the Human Body	22
	The Unbeliever's Response to the Argument from Design	49
CHAPTER FOUR	Morality and Ethics— The Anthropological Argument 59	
	Hedonism	62
	Utilitarianism	63
	Morals/Ethics and the Existence of God	65
	Other Criteria for Establishing the Existence of God	66
	Nihilism	66
	Relativism	67
	Situationism	68
	Determinism	70
	Is There Ultimate Moral Responsibility?	71
CHAPTER FIVE	Conclusion 75	
REFERENCES	 77	

DEDICATION

This volume is dedicated to Winford Claiborne, whose benevolent influence in defense of the Christian faith—by means of the university classroom, printed page, and public radio—will be felt for generations yet to come.

1
INTRODUCTION

One of the most basic, and most fundamental, issues that can be considered by the human mind is the question, "Does God exist?" In the field of logic, there are principles—or as they are called more often, laws—that govern human thought processes and that are accepted as analytically true. One of these is the law of the excluded middle. When applied to objects, this law states that an object cannot both possess and not possess a certain trait or characteristic at the same time and in the same fashion. When applied to propositions, this law states that all precisely-stated propositions are either true or false; they cannot be both true and false at the same time and in the same fashion.

The statement, "God exists," is a precisely-stated proposition. Thus, it is either true or false. The simple fact is, either God exists or He does not. There is no middle ground. One cannot affirm logically both the existence and nonexistence of God. The atheist boldly states that God does not exist; the theist affirms just as boldly that God does exist; the agnostic laments that there is not enough evidence to make a decision on the matter; and the skeptic doubts that God's existence can be proven with certainty. Who is correct? Does God exist or not? The only way to answer this question, of course, is to seek out and examine the evidence. It is certainly reasonable to suggest that if there is a God, He would make available to us evidence adequate to the task of establishing His existence. But does such evidence exist? And if it does, what is the nature of that evidence?

The theist advocates the view that evidence is available to prove conclusively that God does exist, and that this evidence is adequate to establish beyond reasonable doubt the existence of God. However, when we employ the word "prove," we do not mean that God's existence can be demonstrated scientifically in the same fashion that one might prove that a sack of potatoes weighs ten pounds, or that a human heart has four distinct chambers within it. Such matters as the weight of a sack of vegetables, or the divisions within a muscle, are matters that may be verified empirically using the five senses. While empirical evidence often is quite useful in establishing the validity of a case, it is not the sole means of arriving at proof. For example, legal authorities recognize the validity of a *prima facie* case, which is acknowledged to exist when adequate evidence is available to establish the presumption of a fact that, unless such fact can be refuted, legally stands proven. It is the contention of the theist that there is a vast body of evidence that makes an impregnable *prima facie* case for the existence of God—a case that simply cannot be refuted. We would like to present here the *prima facie* case for the existence of God, and a portion of the evidence upon which that case is based.

2
Cause and Effect—
The Cosmological Argument

Throughout human history, one of the most effective arguments for the existence of God has been the cosmological argument, which addresses the fact that the Universe (cosmos) is here and therefore must be explained in some fashion. In his book, *Not A Chance*, R.C. Sproul observed:

> Traditional philosophy argued for the existence of God on the foundation of the law of causality. The cosmological argument went from the presence of a cosmos back to a creator of the cosmos. It sought a rational answer to the question, "Why is there something rather than nothing?" It sought a sufficient reason for a real world (1994, p. 169, emp. in orig.).

The Universe exists and is real. Atheists and agnostics not only acknowledge its existence, but admit that it is a grand effect (e.g., see Jastrow, 1977, pp. 19-21). If an entity cannot account for its own being (i.e., it is not sufficient to have caused itself), then it is said to be "contingent" because it is dependent upon something outside of itself to explain its existence. The Universe is a contingent entity, since it is inadequate to cause, or explain, its own existence. Sproul has

- 3 -

noted: "Logic requires that if something exists contingently, it must have a cause. That is merely to say, if it is an effect it must have an antecedent cause" (1994, p. 172). Thus, since the Universe is a contingent effect, the obvious question becomes, "What **caused** the Universe?"

It is here that the law of cause and effect (also known as the law of causality) is strongly tied to the cosmological argument. Simply put, the law of causality states that every material effect must have an adequate antecedent cause. Just as the law of the excluded middle is analytically true, so the law of cause and effect is analytically true as well. Sproul addressed this when he wrote:

> The statement "Every effect has an antecedent cause" is **analytically true**. To say that it is analytically or formally true is to say that it is true by definition or analysis. There is nothing in the predicate that is not already contained by resistless logic in the subject. It is like the statement, "A bachelor is an unmarried man" or "A triangle has three sides" or "Two plus two are four...." Cause and effect, though distinct ideas, are inseparably bound together in rational discourse. It is meaningless to say that something is a **cause** if it yields no **effect**. It is likewise meaningless to say that something is an **effect** if it has no **cause**. A cause, by definition, must have an effect, or it is not a cause. An effect, by definition, must have a cause, or it is not an effect (1994, pp. 172,171 emp. in orig.).

Effects without adequate causes are unknown. Further, causes never occur subsequent to the effect. It is meaningless to speak of a cause following an effect, or an effect preceding a cause. In addition, the effect is never qualitatively superior to, or quantitatively greater than, the cause. This knowledge is responsible for our formulation of the law of causality in these words: Every material effect must have an **adequate** antecedent cause. The river did not turn muddy because the frog jumped in; the book did not fall from the table because the fly lighted on it. These are not adequate causes. For whatever effects we observe, we must postulate adequate antecedent causes—which brings us back to the original question: What caused the Universe?

There are but three possible answers to this question: (1) the Universe is eternal; it has always existed, and will always exist; (2) the Universe is not eternal; rather, it created itself out of nothing; (3) the Universe is not eternal, and did not create itself out of nothing; rather, it was created by something (or Someone) anterior, and superior, to itself. These three options merit serious consideration.

Is the Universe Eternal?

The most comfortable position for the person who does not believe in God is the idea that the Universe is eternal, because it avoids the problem of a beginning or ending, and thus the need for any "first cause" such as God. In fact, it was to avoid just such a problem that evolutionists Thomas Gold, Hermann Bondi, and Fred Hoyle developed the Steady State Theory. Information had come to light that indicated the Universe was expanding. These scientists suggested that at points in space called "irtrons" hydrogen was coming into existence **from nothing**. As hydrogen atoms arrived, they had to "go" somewhere, and as they did, they displaced matter already in existence, causing the Universe to expand. Dr. Hoyle suggested that the atoms of gaseous hydrogen gradually condensed into clouds of virgin matter, that within these clouds new stars and galaxies formed, etc.

However, the Steady State Theory was doomed to failure, in part, because it violated one of the most fundamental laws of science—the first law of thermodynamics (also referred to as the law of the conservation of matter and/or energy), which states that neither matter nor energy may be created or destroyed in nature. Astronomer Robert Jastrow observed:

> But the creation of matter out of nothing would violate a cherished concept in science—the principle of the

conservation of matter and energy—which states that matter and energy can be neither created nor destroyed. Matter can be converted into energy, and vice versa, but the total amount of all matter and energy in the Universe must remain unchanged forever. It is difficult to accept a theory that violates such a firmly established scientific fact (1977, p. 32).

The Steady State Theory eventually was relegated to the relic heaps of history. Yet problems for those who advocated an eternal Universe continued to multiply because such a concept violated the second law of thermodynamics as well. Simply stated, the second law of thermodynamics dictates that as energy is employed to perform work, it is transformed from a usable to a nonusable form. The Universe is "running down" because energy is becoming less available for use. As Jastrow has remarked:

> And concurrently there was a great deal of discussion about the fact that the second law of thermodynamics, applied to the Cosmos, indicates that the Universe is running down like a clock. If it is running down, there must have been a time when it was fully wound up. Arthur Eddington, the most distinguished astronomer of his day, wrote: "If our views are right, somewhere between the beginning of time and the present day we must place the winding up of the universe." When that occurred, and Who or what wound up the Universe, were questions that bemused theologians, physicists and astronomers, particularly in the 1920's and 1930's (1978, pp. 48-49).

A year before making that admission, Dr. Jastrow made another important concession when he wrote:

> Only as a result of the most recent discoveries can we say with a fair degree of confidence that the world has not existed forever;... The lingering decline predicted by astronomers for the end of the world differs from the explosive conditions they have calculated for its birth, but the impact is the same; **modern science denies an eternal existence to the Universe**, either in the past or in the future (1977, pp. 19,30, emp. added).

The scientific evidence states clearly that the Universe had a beginning—something eternal things do not have. Nor do eternal things "run down," yet clearly the Universe is doing just that, as Dr. Jastrow has stated. As Henry Morris has commented, "The Second Law requires the universe to have had a beginning" (1974, p. 26). Indeed, it does. The Universe now is known not to be eternal.

Did the Universe Create Itself Out of Nothing?

In the past, it would have been practically impossible to find any reputable scientist who would be willing to advocate a self-created Universe. George Davis, a prominent physicist of the past generation, explained why when he wrote: "No material thing can create itself." Further, Dr. Davis affirmed that this statement "cannot be logically attacked on the basis of any knowledge available to us" (1958, p. 71). The Universe is the created, not the creator.

However, as surprising as it may seem, some in the scientific and philosophical communities have stepped forward to defend the option that the Universe simply created itself out of nothing. Edward P. Tryon, professor of physics at the City University of New York, wrote for example: "In 1973, I proposed that our Universe had been created spontaneously from nothing, as a result of established principles of physics. This proposal variously struck people as preposterous, enchanting, or both" (1984, p. 14). But the real push for the acceptance of a self-created Universe came as a result of the work of two physicists, Alan Guth and Paul Steinhardt. In an article titled "The Inflationary Universe," published in the May 1984 issue of *Scientific American*, these two evolutionists wrote:

> From a historical point of view, probably the most revolutionary aspect of the inflationary model is the notion that all the matter and energy in the observable universe may have emerged from almost nothing.... The inflationary model of the universe provides a possible mecha-

nism by which the observed universe could have evolved from an infinitesimal region. It is then tempting to go one step further and speculate that **the entire Universe evolved from literally nothing** (1984, p. 128, emp. added).

Ultimately, the Guth/Steinhardt inflationary model was shown to be incorrect, and a newer version was suggested. Working independently, Russian physicist Andrei Linde, and American physicists Andreas Albrecht and Paul Steinhardt, developed what came to be known as the "new inflationary model" (see Hawking, 1988, pp. 131-132). This model was later shown to be incorrect as well, and eventually was discarded. Later, Linde himself suggested numerous modifications to it, and is credited for producing what is now known as the "chaotic inflationary model" (see Hawking, 1988, pp. 132ff.). Additional work on this particular model was performed by renowned astrophysicist Stephen W. Hawking of Great Britain.

Such ideas as those set forth by Tryon, Guth, Steinhardt, Linde, Albrecht, Hawking, and others have set off a wave of controversy within the scientific community, as is evident from heated discussions at annual scientific meetings, articles published in refereed scientific journals, books written on a scholarly level, and even items appearing in popular science magazines. For example, in the summer 1994 edition of the *Skeptical Inquirer*, Ralph Estling of Great Britain wrote a stinging rebuke of the idea that the Universe created itself out of nothing. Estling suggested:

> The problem emerges in science when scientists leave the realm of science and enter that of philosophy and metaphysics, too often grandiose names for mere personal opinion, untrammeled by empirical evidence or logical analysis, and wearing the mask of deep wisdom. And so they conjure us an entire Cosmos, or myriads of cosmoses, suddenly, inexplicably, causelessly leaping into being out of—out of Nothing Whatsoever, for no reason at all, and thereafter expanding faster than light

into more Nothing Whatsoever.... They then intone equations and other ritual mathematical formulae and look upon it and pronounce it good. I do not think that what these cosmologists, these quantum theorists, these universe-makers, are doing is science. I can't help feeling that universes are notoriously disinclined to spring into being, ready-made, out of nothing (1994, 18[4]: 430).

Estling's article provoked numerous letters to the editor of the *Skeptical Inquirer*, which were printed, with Estling's response, in the January/February 1995 issue. Estling wrote, in part: "All things begin with speculation, science not excluded. But if no empirical evidence is eventually forthcoming, or can be forthcoming, all speculation is barren.... There is no evidence, so far, that the entire universe, observable and unobservable, emerged from a state of absolute Nothingness" (1995, 19[1]:69-70).

Estling is correct, of course. There is no evidence that would allow matter or energy simply to "pop into existence" of its own accord. This point has even been made by physicist Alan Guth, the developer of the original inflationary model. In an interview conducted on June 8, 1994 dealing with the various inflationary models, Dr. Guth conceded:

> First of all, I will say that at the purely technical level, inflation itself does not explain how the universe arose from nothing.... Inflation itself takes a very small universe and produces from it a very big universe. But inflation by itself does not explain where that very small universe came from (as quoted in Heeren, 1995, p. 148).

To suggest that matter/energy can "evolve from literally nothing" would be a clear violation of the first law of thermodynamics. Furthermore, to suggest that the Universe created itself is to posit a self-contradictory position. Sproul addressed this when he wrote that what an atheist or agnostic

> ...deems possible for the world to do—come into being without a cause—is something no judicious philosopher would grant that even God could do. It is as formally and

rationally impossible for God to come into being without a cause as it is for the world to do so.... For something to bring itself into being it must have the power of being within itself. It must at least have enough causal power to cause its own being. If it derives its being from some other source, then it clearly would not be either self-existent or self-created. It would be, plainly and simply, an effect. Of course, the problem is complicated by the other necessity we've labored so painstakingly to establish: It would have to have the causal power of being before it was. It would have to have the power of being before it had any being with which to exercise that power (1994, pp. 179,180).

Science is based on observation and reproducibility. But when pressed for the reproducible, empirical data that document their claim of a self-created Universe, scientists and philosophers are at a loss to produce those data. Perhaps this is why Alan Guth lamented: "In the end, I must admit that questions of plausibility are not logically determinable and depend somewhat on intuition" (1988, 11[2]:76)—which is little more than a fancy way of saying, "I certainly **wish** this were true, but I could not **prove** it to you if my life depended on it." The Universe did not create itself. Such an idea is absurd, both philosophically and scientifically.

Was the Universe Created?

Either the Universe had a beginning, or it did not. But all available evidence indicates that the Universe did have a beginning. If the Universe had a beginning, it either had a cause or it did not. One thing we know assuredly, however: it is correct—logically and scientifically—to acknowledge that the Universe had a cause, because the Universe is an effect, and requires an adequate antecedent cause. Nothing causeless happens.

Since it is apparent that the Universe it not eternal, and since likewise it is apparent that the Universe could not have created itself, the only remaining alternative is that the Universe **was created** by something, or Someone, that: (a) existed before it, i.e., some eternal, uncaused First Cause; (b) is superior to it—since the created cannot be superior to the creator; and (c) is of a different nature, since the finite, contingent Universe of matter is unable to explain itself.

In connection with this, another important fact should be considered. If there had ever been a time when **nothing** existed, then there would be nothing now. It is a self-evident truth that nothing produces nothing. In view of this, **since something exists now, it must follow logically that something has existed forever.** As Sproul has remarked:

> Indeed, reason demands that if something exists, either the world or God (or anything else), then **something must be self-existent.** There must be a self existent being of some sort somewhere, or nothing would or could exist (1994, pp. 179,185, emp. in orig.).

Everything that exists can be classified as either **matter** (which includes energy), or **mind**. There is no third alternative. The theist's argument, then, is this:

1. Everything that exists is either matter or mind.
2. Something exists now, so something eternal must exist.
3. Therefore, either matter or mind is eternal.

A. Either matter or mind is eternal.
B. Matter is not eternal, as per the evidence cited above.
C. Thus, it is mind that is eternal.

In the past, atheists suggested that the mind is nothing more than a function of the brain, which is matter; thus the mind and the brain are the same, and matter is all that exists. However, that viewpoint no longer is intellectually credible, as a result of the experiments of British neurologist, Sir John Eccles. Dr.

Eccles won the Nobel Prize for distinguishing that the mind is more than merely physical. He showed that the supplementary motor area of the brain may be fired by mere **intention** to do something, without the motor cortex of the brain (which controls muscle movements) operating. In effect, the mind is to the brain what a librarian is to a library. The former is not reducible to the latter. Eccles explained his methodology in *The Self and Its Brain*, co-authored with the renowned philosopher of science, Sir Karl Popper (see Popper and Eccles, 1977). In a discussion centering on Dr. Eccles' work, Norman Geisler discussed the concept of an eternal, all-knowing Mind.

> Further, this infinite cause of all that is must be all-knowing. It must be knowing because knowing beings exist. I am a knowing being, and I know it.... But a cause can communicate to its effect only what it has to communicate. If the effect actually possesses some characteristic, then this characteristic is properly attributed to its cause. The cause cannot give what it does not have to give. If my mind or ability to know is received, then there must be Mind or Knower who gave it to me. The intellectual does not arise from the nonintellectual; something cannot arise from nothing (1976, p. 247).

From evidence such as that presented here, Robert Jastrow (an agnostic, by his own admission) was forced to conclude: "That there are what I or anyone would call supernatural forces at work is now, I think, a scientifically proven fact" (1982, p. 18). The evidence speaks clearly regarding the existence of a non-contingent, eternal, self-existent Mind that created this Universe and everything within it.

The law of cause and effect, and the cosmological argument based upon that law, have serious implications in every field of human endeavor. The Universe is here, and must have an adequate antecedent cause. In addressing this problem, R.L. Wysong commented:

> Everyone concludes naturally and comfortably that highly ordered and designed items (machines, houses, etc.) owe existence to a designer. It is unnatural to

conclude otherwise. But evolution asks us to break stride from what is natural to believe and then believe in that which is unnatural, unreasonable, and...unbelievable.... The basis for this departure from what is natural and reasonable to believe is not fact, observation, or experience but rather unreasonable extrapolations from abstract probabilities, mathematics, and philosophy (1976, p. 412, first ellipsis in orig.).

Dr. Wysong presented an interesting historical case to illustrate his point. Some years ago, scientists were called to Great Britain to study orderly patterns of concentric rocks and holes—a find designated as Stonehenge. As studies progressed, it became apparent that these patterns had been designed specifically to allow certain astronomical predictions. Many questions (e.g., how ancient peoples were able to construct an astronomical observatory, how the data derived from their studies were used, etc.) remain unsolved. But one thing is known—the **cause** of Stonehenge was intelligent design.

Now, Wysong suggested, compare Stonehenge to the situation paralleling the origin of the Universe, and of life itself. We study life, observe its functions, contemplate its complexity (which defies duplication even by intelligent men with the most advanced methodology and technology), and what are we to conclude? Stonehenge **might** have been produced by the erosion of a mountain, or by catastrophic natural forces working in conjunction with meteorites to produce rock formations and concentric holes. But what scientist or philosopher would ever suggest such an idea?

No one could ever be convinced that Stonehenge "just happened" by accident, yet atheists and agnostics expect us to believe that this highly-ordered, well-designed Universe, and the complicated life it contains, "just happened." To accept such an idea is, to use Dr. Wysong's words, "to break stride from what is natural to believe" because the conclusion is unreasonable, unwarranted, and unsupported by the facts at hand. The cause simply is not adequate to produce the effect.

The central message of the cosmological argument, and the law of cause and effect upon which it is based, is this: Every material effect must have an adequate antecedent cause. The Universe is here; intelligent life is here; morality is here; love is here. What is their adequate antecedent cause? Since the effect can never precede, or be greater than the cause, it stands to reason that the Cause of life must be a living Intelligence which Itself is both moral and loving. When the Bible records, "In the beginning, God...," it makes known to us just such a First Cause.

3
Design in Nature—
The Teleological Argument

One of the laws of thought employed in the field of logic is the law of rationality, which states that one should accept as true only those conclusions for which there is adequate evidence. This is sensible, because accepting as true a conclusion for which there is no evidence, or inadequate evidence, would be irrational. In establishing the *prima facie* case for the existence of God, theists present—through logic, clear reasoning, and factual data—arguments adequate to justify the acceptance of the conclusion that God exists. The approach is intended to be positive in nature, and to establish a proposition for which adequate evidence is available.

The evidence used to substantiate the theist's proposition concerning God's existence may take many forms. This should not be surprising since, if He does exist, God would be the greatest of all realities. His existence, therefore, could be extrapolated not from just a single line of reasoning, but from numerous avenues. As one writer of the past suggested:

> The reality of such a Being can be firmly established only by concurrent reasons coming from various realms

of existence, and approved by various powers of the human spirit. It is a conclusion that cannot be reached without the aid of arguments inadequate by themselves to so great a result, yet valid in their place, proving each some part of the great truth; proofs cumulative and complementary, each requiring others for its completion (Clarke, 1912, p. 104).

The various arguments presented by theists, all combined, make an ironclad case for God's existence. Where one particular argument fails to impress or convince an inquirer, another may avail. Considered cumulatively, the evidence is adequate to justify the intended conclusion. It is our purpose here to present and discuss additional evidence substantiating the proposition: God exists.

In contending for the existence of God, theists often employ the teleological argument. "Teleology" has reference to purpose or design. Thus, this approach suggests that where there is purposeful design, there must be a designer. The deduction being made, of course, is that order, planning, and design in a system are indicative of intelligence, purpose, and specific intent on the part of the originating cause. In logical form, the theist's argument may be presented as follows:

1. If the Universe evinces purposeful design, there must have been a designer.
2. The Universe does evince purposeful design.
3. Thus, the Universe must have had a designer.

This correct form of logical reasoning, and the implications that flow from it, have not escaped the attention of those who do not believe in God. Atheistic philosopher Paul Ricci has written: "...it's true that everything designed has a designer..." (1986, p. 190). In fact, Mr. Ricci even conceded that the statement, " 'Everything designed has a designer,' is an analytically true statement" and thus requires no formal proof (p. 190). Apparently Mr. Ricci understands that one does not get a poem without a poet, a law without a lawgiver, a painting without a painter, or design without a designer.

He is in good company among his disbelieving counterparts. Evolutionist Richard Lewontin made the following admission in an article he authored for *Scientific American*:

> Life forms are more than simply multiple and diverse, however. Organisms fit remarkably well into the external world in which they live. They have morphologies, physiologies and behaviors that **appear to have been carefully and artfully designed** to enable each organism to appropriate the world around it for its own life. It was the marvelous fit of organisms to the environment, much more than the great diversity of forms, that was **the chief evidence of a Supreme Designer** (1978, 239[3]:213, emp. added).

To be fair to both of these authors, and others like them, let us quickly point out that while they agree with the thrust of the theist's argument (i.e., that design leads inevitably to a designer), they do not believe that there is evidence warranting the conclusion that a Supreme Designer exists, and they therefore have rejected any belief in God. Their disagreement with the theist would center on statement number two (the minor premise) in the above syllogism. While admitting that design demands a designer, they would deny that there is design in nature providing proof of the existence of a Great Designer.

A good example of such a denial can be found in a book written by British evolutionist, Richard Dawkins. During the 1800s, William Paley employed his now-famous "watch argument." Paley argued that if one were to discover a watch lying upon the ground, and were to examine it closely, the design inherent in the watch would be enough to force the conclusion that there must have been a watchmaker. Paley continued his line of argumentation to suggest that the design inherent in the Universe should be enough to force the conclusion that there must have been a Great Designer. In 1986, Dawkins published *The Blind Watchmaker*, which was intended to put to rest once and for all Paley's argument. The dust jacket of Dawkins' book made that point clear:

> There may be good reasons for belief in God, but the argument from design is not one of them. ...despite all appearances to the contrary, there is no watchmaker in nature beyond the blind forces of physics.... Natural selection, the unconscious, automatic, blind yet essentially nonrandom process that Darwin discovered, and that we now understand to be the explanation for the existence and form of all life, has no purpose in mind. It has no mind and no mind's eye. It does not plan for the future. It has no vision, no foresight, no sight at all. If it can be said to play the role of watchmaker in nature, it is the **blind** watchmaker (1986, emp. in orig.).

The disagreement between the theist and atheist is not whether design demands a designer. Rather, the point of contention is whether or not there **is** design in nature adequate to substantiate the conclusion that a Designer does, in fact, exist. This is where the teleological argument is of benefit.

Design of the Universe

Our Universe operates in accordance with exact scientific laws. The precision of the Universe (and the exactness of its laws) allows scientists to launch rockets to the Moon, with the full knowledge that, upon their arrival, they can land within a few feet of their intended target. Such precision and exactness also allow astronomers to predict solar/lunar eclipses years in advance, or to determine when Halley's Comet can be seen once again from the Earth. Science writer Lincoln Barnett once observed:

> This functional harmony of nature Berkeley, Descartes, and Spinoza attributed to God. Modern physicists who prefer to solve their problems without recourse to God (although this seems to be more difficult all the time) emphasize that nature mysteriously operates on mathematical principles. It is the mathematical orthodoxy of the Universe that enables theorists like Einstein to predict and discover natural laws, simply by the solution of equations (1959, p. 22).

The precision, complexity, and orderliness within the Universe are not in dispute; writers such as Jastrow, Ricci, Dawkins, and Lewontin acknowledge as much. But while atheists willingly concede complexity, and even order, they are not prepared to concede design because the implication of such a concession would demand a Designer. Is there evidence of **design**? The atheist claims no such evidence exists. The theist, however, affirms that it does, and offers the following information in support of that affirmation.

We live in a tremendously large Universe. While its outer limits have not been measured, it is estimated to be as much as 20 billion light years in diameter (i.e., the distance it would take light to travel across the Universe at a speed of over 186,000 miles per second; see Lawton, 1981, 89[1]:105). There are an estimated one billion galaxies in the Universe (Lawton, 1981, 89[1]:98), and an estimated 25 sextillion stars. The Milky Way galaxy in which we live contains over 100 billion stars, and is so large that even traveling at the speed of light would require 100,000 years to cross its diameter. Light travels in one year approximately 5.87×10^{12} miles; in 100,000 years, that would be 5.87×10^{17} miles, or 587 quadrillion miles just to cross the diameter of a single galaxy. If we drew a map of the Milky Way galaxy, and represented the Earth and Sun as two dots one inch apart (thus a scale of one inch equals 93 million miles—the distance between the Earth and the Sun), we would need a map at least four miles wide to locate the next nearest star, and a map 25,000 miles wide to reach the center of our galaxy. Without doubt, this is a rather impressive Universe.

Yet while the size itself is impressive, the inherent design is even more so. The Sun's interior temperature is estimated at over 20 million degrees Celsius (Lawton, 1981, 89[1]:102). The Earth, however, is located at exactly the correct distance from the Sun to receive the proper amount of heat and radiation to sustain life as we know it. If the Earth were moved just

10% closer to the Sun (about 10 million miles), far too much heat and radiation would be absorbed. If the Earth were moved just 10% further from the Sun, too little heat would be absorbed. Either scenario would spell doom for life on the Earth.

The Earth is rotating on its axis at 1,000 miles per hour at the equator, and moving around the Sun at 70,000 miles per hour (approximately 19 miles per second), while the Sun and its solar system are moving through space at 600,000 miles per hour in an orbit so large it would take over 220 million years just to complete a single orbit. Interestingly, however, as the Earth moves in its orbit around the Sun, it departs from a straight line by only one-ninth of an inch every eighteen miles. If it departed by one-eighth of an inch, we would come so close to the Sun that we would be incinerated; if it departed by one-tenth of an inch, we would find ourselves so far from the Sun that we would all freeze to death (*Science Digest*, 1981, 89[1]:124). The Earth is poised some 240,000 miles from the Moon, whose gravitational pull produces ocean tides. If the Moon were moved closer to the Earth by just a fifth, the tides would be so enormous that twice a day they would reach 35-50 feet high over most of the Earth's surface.

What would happen if the rotation rate of the Earth were halved, or doubled? If it were halved, the seasons would be doubled in their length, which would cause such harsh heat and cold over much of the Earth that it would be difficult, if not impossible, to grow enough food to feed the Earth's population. If the rotation rate were doubled, the length of each season would be halved, and it would be difficult or impossible to grow enough food to feed the Earth's population. The Earth is tilted on its axis at exactly 23.5 degrees. Were that tilt to be reduced to zero, much of the Earth's water would accumulate around the two poles, leaving vast deserts in their place. If the atmosphere surrounding the Earth were much thinner, meteorites could strike our planet with greater force and frequency, causing worldwide devastation.

The oceans provide a huge reservoir of moisture that is constantly evaporating and condensing, thus falling upon the land as refreshing rain. It is a well-known fact that water heats and cools at a much slower rate than a solid land mass, which explains why desert regions can be blistering hot in the daytime and freezing cold at night. But water holds its temperature longer, providing a natural heating/air-conditioning system for the land areas of the Earth. Temperature extremes would be much more erratic than they are, were it not for the fact that approximately four-fifths of the Earth is covered with water. In addition, humans and animals inhale oxygen and exhale carbon dioxide. On the other hand, plants take in carbon dioxide and give off oxygen. We depend upon the world of botany for our oxygen supply, yet approximately 90% of that oxygen comes from microscopic plants in the seas (see Asimov, 1975, 2:116). If our oceans were appreciably smaller, we would soon be out of air to breathe.

Can a person reasonably be expected to believe that these exacting requirements for life have been met "by accident"? The Earth is exactly the right distance from the Sun; it is exactly the right distance from the Moon; it has exactly the right diameter; it has exactly the right atmospheric pressure; it has exactly the right tilt; it has exactly the right amount of oceanic water; it has exactly the right weight and mass; and so on. Were this many requirements to be met in any other essential area of life, the idea that they had been provided "by accident" would be dismissed as ludicrous. Yet atheists and agnostics suggest that the Universe, the Earth, and life itself are all here as a result of fortuitous accidents. Physicist John Gribbin (1983), writing on the requirements necessary for life on Earth, emphasized both the nature and essentiality of those requirements, yet chose to title his article, "Earth's Lucky Break"—as if the precision, orderliness, and intricate design of the Universe could be explained by postulating that the Earth received, in a roll of the cosmic dice, a "lucky break,"

For more than a decade-and-a-half, British evolutionist Sir Fred Hoyle has stressed the insurmountable problems with such thinking, and has addressed specifically the difficulty faced by those who defend the idea of a naturalistic origin of life on Earth. In fact, Dr. Hoyle described the atheistic concept that disorder gives rise to order in a rather picturesque manner when he observed that "the chance that higher forms have emerged in this way is comparable with the chance that a tornado sweeping through a junk-yard might assemble a Boeing 747 from the materials therein" (1981a, p. 105). Dr. Hoyle even went so far as to draw the following conclusion:

> Once we see, however, that the probability of life originating at random is so utterly miniscule as to make the random concept absurd, it becomes sensible to think that the favourable properties of physics on which life depends, are in every respect deliberate.... It is therefore almost inevitable that our own measure of intelligence must reflect in a valid way the higher intelligences... even to the extreme idealized limit of **God** (Hoyle and Wickramasinghe, 1981, pp. 141,144, emp. in orig.).

Atheist Richard Dawkins was forced to admit: "The more statistically improbable a thing is, the less we can believe that it just happened by blind chance. Superficially, **the obvious alternative to chance is an intelligent Designer**" (1982, p. 130, emp. added). That is the very conclusion theists have drawn from the available evidence—in keeping with the law of rationality. The statistical improbability of the Universe "just happening by blind chance" is staggering. The only alternative is an Intelligent Designer—God.

Design of the Human Body

Many years ago, the ancient scholar, Augustine, observed that "Men go abroad to wonder at the height of mountains, at the huge waves of the sea, at the long course of the rivers, at the vast compass of the ocean, at the circular motion of the stars; and they pass by themselves without wondering." Indeed, while we stand in amazement at so many stunning scenes from our unique Universe, we often fail to stand equally amazed at the marvelous creation of man. According to those who do not believe in God, the human body is little more than the result of a set of fortuitous circumstances credited to that mythical lady, "mother nature." Yet such a suggestion does not fit the actual facts of the case, as even evolutionists have been forced to recognize from time to time. The late George Gaylord Simpson of Harvard once suggested that in man one finds "the most highly endowed organization of matter that has yet appeared on the earth..." (1949, p. 293). Another evolutionist observed:

> When you come right down to it, the most incredible creation in the universe is you—with your fantastic senses and strengths, your ingenious defense systems, and mental capabilities so great you can never use them to the fullest. Your body is a structural masterpiece more amazing than science fiction (Guinness, 1987, p. 5).

Can one reasonably be expected to conclude that the "structural masterpiece" of the human body—with its "ingenious" systems and "highly endowed organization"—is the result of blind chance operating over eons of time in nature as atheism suggests? Or would it be more in keeping with the facts of the matter to suggest that the human body is the result of purposeful design by a Master Designer?

For organizational purposes, the human body may be considered at four different levels. First, there are cells, representing the smallest unit of life. Second, there are tissues (muscle tissue, nerve tissue, etc.), which are groups of the same kind of cells carrying on the same kind of activity. Third, there are organs (heart, liver, etc.), which are groups of tissues working together in unison. Fourth, there are systems (reproductive system, circulatory system, etc.), which are composed of groups of organs carrying out specific bodily functions. To the unbiased, it should be obvious that the physical body has been marvelously designed and intricately organized for the purpose of facilitating human existence upon the Earth. While we will not have the space here to examine each of them, an investigation of the body's various levels of organization, and of the body as a whole, leads inescapably to the conclusion that there is intelligent design at work, as the following facts clearly attest.

The Body's Cells

A human body is composed of over 30 different kinds of cells (red blood cells, white blood cells, nerve cells, etc.), totaling approximately 100 trillion cells in an average adult (Beck, 1971, p. 189). These cells come in a variety of sizes and shapes, with different functions and life expectancies. For example, some cells (e.g., male spermatazoa) are so small that 20,000 would fit inside a capital "O" from a standard typewriter, each being only 0.05 mm long. Some cells, placed end-to-end, would make only one inch if 6,000 were assembled together. Yet all the cells of the human body, if set end-to-end, would encircle the Earth over 200 times. Even the largest cell of the human body, the female ovum, is unbelievably small, being only 0.01 of an inch in diameter.

Cells have three major components. First, each cell is composed of a cell membrane that encloses the organism. Second, inside the cell is a three-dimensional cytoplasm—a watery matrix containing specialized organelles. Third, within the cytoplasm is the nucleus, which contains most of the genetic material, and which serves as the control center of the cell.

The lipoprotein cell membrane (lipids/proteins/lipids) is approximately 0.06-0.08 of a micrometer thick, yet allows selective transport into, and out of, the cell. Evolutionist Ernest Borek has observed: "The membrane recognizes with its uncanny molecular memory the hundreds of compounds swimming around it and permits or denies passage according to the cell's requirements" (1973, p. 5).

Inside the cytoplasm, there are over 20 different chemical reactions occurring at any one time, with each cell containing five major components for: (1) communication; (2) waste disposal; (3) nutrition; (4) repair; and (5) reproduction. Within this watery matrix there are such organelles as the mitochondria (over 1,000 per cell in many instances) that provide the cell with its energy. The endoplasmic reticulum is a "...transport system designed to carry materials from one part of the cell to the other" (Pfeiffer, 1964, p. 13). Ribosomes are miniature protein-producing factories. Golgi bodies store the proteins manufactured by the ribosomes. Lysozomes within the cytoplasm function as garbage disposal units.

The nucleus is the control center of the cell, and is separated from the cytoplasm by a nuclear membrane. Within the nucleus is the genetic machinery of the cell (chromosomes and genes containing deoxyribonucleic acid—DNA). The DNA is a supermolecule that carries the coded information for the replication of the cell. If the DNA from a single human cell were removed from the nucleus and unraveled (it is found in the cell in a spiral configuration), it would be approximately six feet long, and would contain over a billion biochemical steps. It has been estimated that if all the DNA in an adult human were placed end-to-end, it would reach to the Sun and back (186 million miles) 400 times.

It should also be noted that the DNA molecule does something that we as humans have yet to accomplish: it stores coded information in a chemical format, and then uses a biologic agent (RNA) to decode and activate it. As Darrel Kautz has stated: "Human technology has not yet advanced to the point of storing information **chemically** as it is in the DNA molecule" (1988, p. 45, emp. in orig.; see also Jackson, 1993, pp. 11-12). If transcribed into English, the DNA in a single human cell would fill a 1,000 volume set of encyclopedias approximately 600 pages each (Gore, 1976, p. 357). Yet just as amazing is the fact that all the genetic information needed to reproduce the entire human population (about five billion people) could be placed into a space of about one-eighth of a square inch. In comparing the amount of information contained in the DNA molecule with a much larger computer microchip, evolutionist Irvin Block remarked: "We marvel at the feats of memory and transcription accomplished by computer microchips, but these are gargantuan compared to the protein granules of deoxyribonucleic acid, DNA" (1980, p. 52).

In an article written for *Encyclopaedia Britannica*, Carl Sagan observed that "the information content of a simple cell has been estimated as around 10^{12} bits [i.e., one trillion—BT/WJ]..." (1974, 10:894). To emphasize to the reader the enormity of this figure, Dr. Sagan then noted that if one were to count every letter in every word of every book in the world's largest library (over ten million volumes), the final tally would be approximately a trillion letters. Thus, a single cell contains the equivalent information content of every book in the world's largest library of more than ten million volumes! Every rational person recognizes that not one of the books in such a library "just happened." Rather, each and every one is the result of intelligence and painstaking **design**.

What, then, may we say about the infinitely more complex genetic code found within the DNA in each cell? Sir Fred Hoyle concluded that the notion that such complexity could be arrived at by chance is "nonsense of a high order" (1981b, p. 527). In their text on the origin of life, Thaxton, Bradley, and Olsen addressed the implications of the genetic code.

> We know that in numerous cases certain effects always have intelligent causes, such as dictionaries, sculptures, machines and paintings. We reason by analogy that similar effects have intelligent causes. For example, after looking up to see "BUY FORD" spelled out in smoke across the sky we infer the presence of a skywriter even if heard or saw no airplane. We would similarly conclude the presence of intelligent activity were we to come upon an elephant-shaped topiary in a cedar forest.

> In like manner an intelligible communication via radio signal from some distant galaxy would be widely hailed as evidence of an intelligent source. Why then doesn't the message sequence on the DNA molecule also constitute *prima facie* evidence for an intelligent source? After all, DNA information is not just analogous to a message sequence such as Morse code, it **is** such a message sequence....
>
> We believe that if this question is considered, it will be seen that most often it is answered in the negative simply because it is thought to be inappropriate to bring a Creator into science (1984, pp. 211-212, emp. in orig.).

The intricate and complex nature of the DNA molecule—combined with the staggering amount of chemically-coded information that it contains—speaks unerringly to the fact that this "supermolecule" simply could not have come into existence due to blind chance and random natural forces operating through eons of time, as evolutionists have claimed. This is not an adequate explanation for the inherent complexity of the DNA molecule. Andrews was correct when he stated:

> It is not possible for a code, of any kind, to arise by chance or accident.... A code is the work of an intelligent mind. Even the cleverest dog or chimpanzee could not work out a code of any kind. It is obvious then that chance cannot do it.... This could no more have been the work of chance or accident than could the "Moonlight Sonata" be played by mice running up and down the keyboard of my piano! Codes do not arise from chaos (1978, pp. 28-29).

Indeed, codes do not arise from chaos. When Dawkins suggested that "**superficially,** the obvious alternative to chance is an intelligent Designer," obviously he intended his comment as a somewhat satirical insult aimed at theists who were capable of thinking only "superficially" (1982, p. 130, emp. added). However, it is hardly superficial to suggest that obvious design demands a designer. In fact, that is the exact point the theist is stressing: an intelligent Designer is demanded by the evidence.

The Body's Tissues

In the human body, there are numerous tissues (e.g., muscle tissues, nerve tissues, etc.). In fact, a single human has more than 600 muscles (containing about six billion muscle fibers), composing about 40% of the body's weight. According to Dr. I. MacKay Murray, professor of anatomy at the State University of New York, muscles are the "engines" of the body that provide the power for movement (1969, p. 22). Some muscles are tiny, such as those regulating the amount of light entering the eye, while others, like those in the legs, are massive.

Muscles may be classified either as "voluntary" (i.e., under the control of the human will), or "involuntary" (i.e., not under control of the will). The voluntary muscles of the arms, for example, are attached to the bones by tough cords of connective tissue called tendons. One must "think" in order to move these muscles. The involuntary muscles are those whose contraction and relaxation cannot be controlled consciously (e.g., the heart and intestines). Some muscles are both voluntary and involuntary (e.g., the muscles controlling the eyelids, and the diaphragm). All muscles, in one way or another, are regulated by the nervous system.

Muscles work by contracting (tightening). When they contract, they shorten, thus exerting a "pull"; muscles do not "push." Frequently, muscles work in pairs, as in the voluntary skeletal muscles. The biceps in the upper arm pulls the forearm forward, whereas the triceps moves the forearm downward. While one works, the other rests. The design inherent in such tissues is utterly amazing.

Some muscles, like those attached to the skeleton, are analogous to strong steel cables. Each muscle is constructed of long cells combined in small bundles called fibers. These bundles are bound together, making larger bundles of which the whole muscle consists. Muscle fibers vary in size from a few hundred-thousandths of an inch, to an inch or inch-and-a-half in length. Each muscle has its own stored supply of high-grade fuel, especially sugar (glycogen), which the body has manufactured from food that has been consumed. This analogy may be helpful. In an automobile engine, the spark ignites vaporized gasoline, the piston moves, and keeps moving in response to a series of explosions. "A muscle performs the functions of both the spark and the piston; the cell itself splits a molecule of fuel and also exerts the resulting physical power" (Miller and Goode, 1960, p. 23). If it is clear that an automobile engine was intelligently designed, why is it not reasonable to draw the same conclusion with reference to muscles. Lenihan, even though an evolutionist, writes: "The body's engines [muscles—BT/WJ]...demonstrate some surprisingly modern engineering ideas" (1974, p. 43). The question is: Who initiated these "engineering ideas"? The answer, of course, is the Great Designer, God.

Connected to the skeletal muscle is a nerve. The nerve conveys a signal telling the muscle when to contract or relax. Obviously, there must be precise orchestration between the skeletal muscle system and the nervous system. Without doubt, their cooperative nature was planned. Some muscles, like those in the stomach, are stimulated to work by means of chemicals call hormones.

Further, there is a precisely-integrated relationship between muscles and bones. Here is just one such example. "As certain muscles increase in strength, they pull harder than before on the bones to which they are attached. With this as a stimulus, bone-forming cells build new bone to give internal reinforcement where necessary" (Shryock, 1968, p. 27). Would this indicate design?

In his book, *Human Design*, evolutionist William S. Beck could hardly contain himself when he wrote of "the intricate structural organization" of the muscles and tendons in the hand, which are capable of such a wide variety of actions. But "intricate structural organization" indicates design. Beck characterized this phenomenon as "one of evolution's most remarkable achievements" (1971, p. 691). Remarkable indeed! A number of years ago, an article on the human hand appeared in the magazine, *Today's Health*, published by the American Medical Association. Though saturated with evolutionary concepts (e.g., the hand is alleged to have evolved from a fish's fin), the article conceded:

> ...If the most gifted scientists cudgeled their brains they probably could not come up with a stronger or more perfect tool for grasping and delicate manipulation than the human hand. And seen **from an engineering standpoint**, the loveliest hand is a highly complex mechanical device composed of muscle, bone, tendon, fat, and extremely sensitive nerve fibers, capable of performing thousands of jobs with precision (Wylie, 1962, p. 25, emp. added).

But something "engineered" requires an **engineer**. That is just sound logic.

While many living organisms share common muscle activity, there are some muscle movements that are unique to man. These forcefully demonstrate that the human being is not some kind of "evolved animal." Rather, he is a creature "fearfully and wonderfully made" by a Creator. Observe the following quotation from two evolutionists, which no doubt reveals more than these authors intended. Then, ask yourself how scientists can echo these sentiments and still ignore the evidence of design in nature that demands a Designer.

> Only man can combine muscle with intelligence and imagination, plan and purpose, to plow and plant a field, to create a museum masterpiece or the "Gettysburg Address." And only man trains to perform the most highly coordinated forms of bodily motion for their own sake, in the expressive and athletic arts. We applaud this skill in our species every time we clap our hands for a ballerina or a circus aerialist (Miller and Goode, 1960, p. 21).

The Body's Organs

The Skin

The skin is the largest single organ of the human body. It consists of three areas: (a) the skin layers; (b) the glands; and (c) the nails. If the skin of a 150-pound man were spread out, it would cover 20 square feet of space and weigh about 9 pounds. The skin is also a very busy area. "A piece of skin the size of a quarter contains 1 yard of blood vessels, 4 yards of nerves, 25 nerve ends, 100 sweat glands, and more than 3 million cells" (Youmans, 1979, 17:404d).

The skin, containing two major layers, is, on average, only about one-eighth of an inch thick. The epidermis is the upper layer, and consists of rows of cells about 12 to 15 deep. The uppermost layers are dead, and are being replaced constantly with newly-formed living cells. It would be an interesting question to ask: What man-made house replaces its own covering? The epidermis contains a pigment called melanin, which gives the skin its distinctive color. The lower layer is designated as the dermis, and is joined to the epidermis by a corrugated surface that contains nerves and blood vessels. When a cut finger draws blood, the dermis has been reached. Within the dermis there are two kinds of glands—sweat and oil.

The ends of the fingers and toes are protected by a horn-like substance, usually referred to as the toenail or fingernail. Actually, most of the nail is dead; only the lower, crescent-shaped, white portion is living. The fingernails grow about three times as fast as the toenails, which is certainly evidence of good design, considering the respective functions of the hands and feet. The skin of the underside of the fingers, the palms, and the soles of the feet have a special friction surface, and no hair. These areas, like the knurling on a tool handle or the tread of a tire, have been designed specifically for gripping (see Miller and Goode, 1960, p. 345).

Hair has several functions. It is a part of the body's sentry system. Eyelashes warn the eyes to close when foreign objects strike them. Body hairs also serve as levers, connected to muscles, to help squeeze the oil glands. Hair acts as a filter in the ears and nose. Hair grows to a certain length, falls out, and then, in most instances, is replaced by new hair. Hair is "programmed" to grow only to a certain length. But who provided the "program"? Compared to most mammals, man is relatively hairless. But why is this the case? A strong case can be made for the fact that the best explanation is to be found "in the design of the human body with personhood in view" (Cosgrove, 1987, p. 54). Skin touch is very closely associated with human emotions.

Human skin is one of the body's most vital organs. Its value may be summarized as follows.

(1) The skin is a protective fortification that keeps harmful bacteria from entering the human system.

(2) It is a waterproof wall that holds in the fluids of the body. Our bodies are about 75% fluid.

(3) It protects the interior parts of the body from cuts, bruises, etc.

(4) With its pigment, melanin, it shields the body from harmful rays arriving on the Earth from the Sun. Beck calls melanin "an epidermal light filter" (1971, p. 745). Do light filters invented by man require intelligence?

(5) The skin's many nerve endings make it sensitive to touch, cold, heat, pain, and pressure. Thus, it is a major sense organ.

(6) The sweat glands (2 to 5 million in the whole body) help eliminate waste products and also function in cooling the skin.

(7) The oil glands lubricate the skin and help keep it soft—while at the same time providing a waterproofing system. Though soft, the skin is quite durable. When a 2,000-year-old Egyptian mummy was fingerprinted, the ridges were found to be perfectly preserved (Guinness, 1987, p. 132).

(8) About one-third of the body's blood circulates through the skin. The blood vessels, by contracting and expanding, work to regulate body temperature. If body temperature increases by 7 or 8 degrees, and remains there for any length of time, a person almost always will die. The skin is thus a radiator system (see Brand and Yancey, 1980, p. 154). Does a radiator happen by accident?

(9) The skin absorbs ultraviolet rays from the Sun, and uses them to convert chemicals into vitamin D, which the body needs for the utilization of calcium. The skin is therefore a chemical-processing plant for the entire body.

The Eye

One of the most forceful evidences of design within the human body is the eye. Even Charles Darwin struggled with the problem of an organ so complex as the eye evolving via naturalistic processes. In *The Origin of Species* he wrote:

> To suppose that the eye with all its inimitable contrivances for adjusting the focus to different distances, for admitting different amounts of light, and for the correction of spherical and chromatic aberration, could have been formed by natural selection, seems, I freely confess, absurd in the highest sense (1859, p. 170).

However, in spite of his misgivings, Darwin went on to argue that the eye had, in fact, been produced by natural selection through an evolutionary process. Darwin, of course, is not the only one to be troubled by what appears to be obvious evidence of design in the eye. Evolutionist Robert Jastrow has written:

> The eye is a marvelous instrument, resembling a telescope of the highest quality, with a lens, an adjustable focus, a variable diaphragm for controlling the amount of light, and optical corrections for spherical and chromatic aberration. **The eye appears to have been designed; no designer of telescopes could have done better.** How could this marvelous instrument have evolved by chance, through a succession of random events? (1981, pp. 96-97, emp. added).

Though Dr. Jastrow argued that "the fact of evolution is not in doubt," he nonetheless confessed: "...there seems to be no direct proof that evolution can work these miracles.... **It is hard to accept the evolution of the eye as a product of chance**" (1981, pp. 101,97,98, emp. added).

Considering how extremely complex the mechanism of the eye is known to be, it is easy to understand why Dr. Jastrow would make such a comment. Light images from the environment enter the eye (at approximately 186,000 miles per second) through the iris, which opens and shuts like the diaphragm of a camera, to let in just the right amount of light. The images move through a lens that focuses the "picture" (in an inverted form) on the retina at the rear of the eyeball. The image is then picked up by some 137 million nerve endings that convey the message (at over 300 miles per hour) to the brain for processing. Little wonder that secular writers are prone to speak of "the miraculous teamwork of your eye and your brain" (Guinness, 1987, p. 196). In fact, the vocabulary of such writers becomes rather unguarded when contemplating this phenomenon. Bioengineer John Lenihan has suggested: "The eye is an exceptionally sensitive optical instrument **displaying many striking features of design** and performance; even the windscreen washers and wipers have not been forgotten" (1974, p. 75, emp. added). Since Dr. Lenihan is an evolutionist, his terminology cannot be dismissed as some kind of creationist jargon.

The eye frequently is compared to a camera. Evolutionists Miller and Goode have suggested: "The living camera of the eye photographs fleeting images by the thousands, between one moment and the next, and it makes its own adjustments, automatically and precisely, with each change in distance light, and angle" (1960, p. 315). Actually, the camera was patterned after the eye—a fact admitted even by evolutionists. The Time-Life science series volume, *The Body*, spoke of the camera as a "man-made eye" and conceded that this optical instrument was "modeled" after the design of the eye (Nourse, 1964, p. 154). Indeed, the eye does display many striking features of design. The eye is infinitely more complex than any man-made camera. It can handle 1.5 million simultaneous messages, and gathers 80% of all the knowledge absorbed by the brain. The retina covers less than a square inch, and contains 137 million light-sensitive receptor cells, 130 million rods (allowing the eye to see in black and white), and 7 million cones (allowing the eye to see in full color). In an average day, the eye moves about 100,000 times, using muscles that, milligram for milligram, are among the body's strongest. The body would have to walk 50 miles to exercise the leg muscles an equal amount. If the function of the camera demands that it was "made," does it not stand to reason that the more complex human camera, the eye, also must have had a Maker?

The Ear

Another incontrovertible evidence of design within the human body is the ear, which is composed of three areas: outer, middle, and inner. Sound waves enter the outer ear (at a speed of 1,087 feet per second) and pass along a tube to the middle ear. Stretched across the tube is a thin membrane, the eardrum. The sound waves hit this tissue and cause it to vibrate. The resulting vibrations then are conveyed into the inner ear where they in turn vibrate three small bones— the hammer, anvil, and stirrup (popular names derived from the shape of these bones) that are joined together and operated by tiny muscles. The result is that the sound is amplified.

These bones, which one authority says "are **designed** to transmit even very faint sounds," (Sedeen, 1986, p. 280, emp. added), are connected to another membrane called the oval window. As the oval window vibrates, it generates movement within a small spiral passage, the cochlea, which is filled with liquid. The vibrations within the cochlea are picked up by some 25,000 auditory receptors and transferred as electrical impulses, by means of the auditory nerve (with its 30,000 nerve fibers) to the brain. The brain receives these vibrations (up to 25,000 per second) and interprets them as voice, thunder, music (more than 1,500 separate musical tones), or as the thousands of other sounds that we hear daily. The complexity of this integrated system is nothing short of amazing. One writer noted: "Amazingly, the inner ear, although no bigger than a hazelnut, contains as many circuits as the telephone system of a good-sized city" (Guinness, 1987, p. 208). Would anyone suggest that a city's telephone system could design itself? Dr. Lenihan even went so far as to remark that the "level of sensitivity" within the human ear is "far beyond the achievement of any microphone" and "represents the ultimate limit of performance" (1974, p. 87).

The cochlea contains three tubes, called the semi-circular canals, which are partially filled with fluids that move whenever the head moves. Nerve endings from these canals are connected to the brain and this, in cooperation with the muscle system, helps us keep our equilibrium or balance. The balancing ability of the auditory system has been compared to the "inertial system used in missiles and submarines" (Lenihan, 1974, p. 90). Thus, the ear mechanism actually is designed to accomplish two functions—hearing and balance. This feature of the body demonstrates incredible planning. In the words of Lenihan, "The combination, in such a small space, of the hearing and balancing systems of the body **represents a remarkable achievement of biological engineering**" (1974, p. 94, emp. added). Does "blind nature" have the ability to engineer such remarkable technology?

The psalmist affirmed that God "planted the ear" and "formed the eye" (Psalm 94:9). Hearing and seeing are not developments of an eons-long evolutionary process. "The hearing ear, and the seeing eye, Jehovah has made even both of them " (Proverbs 20:12). "Our eyes and ears are transformers. They sense the light and sounds around us and turn them into electrical impulses that the brain can interpret. **Each organ is designed** to handle its own medium" (Sedeen, 1986, p. 276, emp. added). Designed indeed! And such design speaks eloquently of a Grand Designer.

The Body's Systems

The Skeletal System

The average adult has 206 bones in his body (an infant can have up to 350, but many of these fuse during the maturation process). The human skeleton accounts for about 15-20% of the body's weight, with bones serving several important functions.

(1) Bones have been designed to be a rigid support for the organs and tissues of the body. They are like the interior framework of a house. The skeletal system is "something of an **engineering marvel**, strong enough to support weight and carry burdens, yet flexible to cushion shocks and allow for an extraordinary variety of motion" (Miller and Goode, 1960, p. 25, emp. added). Who was the engineer responsible for the marvel known as the skeletal system?

(2) Bones function as protective devices for many of the softer parts of the anatomy. For example, certain sections of the skull, which are independent in infancy but have grown together in the adult, offer protection for the fragile brain. The 12 pairs of ribs form a cage to shield the heart and lungs. The backbone (called the spinal column) is made up of 33 block-like bones that are ingeniously designed to allow movement, yet these bones protect a major feature of the nervous system—the spinal cord.

(3) Bones also serve as levers. Miller and Goode have noted:

> When our muscles move us about, they do it by working a series of articulated levers that make a most efficient use of every ounce of muscular motive power. The levers

are the bones of the body's framework, fitted together with the neatness of jigsaw pieces and hinged by joints that must win the admiration of any mechanic (1960, p. 25).

(4) Bones also have a metabolic function. Until fairly recently, it was assumed that bones were inert tissue. However, studies have revealed that they are "constantly being remodeled" (Beck, 1971, p. 626). They provide a reservoir of essential minerals (99% of the calcium and 88% of the phosphorus, plus other trace elements), which must be rebuilt continuously. For example, without calcium, impulses could not travel along the nerves, and blood would not clot. Too, red blood cells (180 million of which die every sixty seconds), certain white blood cells, and platelets arise in the marrow of the bones. Incredibly, when a bone is broken it immediately begins to repair itself. And, after the repair process is complete, it will be even stronger than it was before. Brand and Yancey have commented:

> Perhaps an engineer will someday develop a substance as strong and light and efficient as bone, but what engineer could devise a substance that, like bone, can grow continuously, lubricate itself, require no shutdown time, and repair itself when damage occurs? (1980, p. 91).

In order for the skeletal system to be effective, it must have several attributes, among which are strength, elasticity, and lightness of weight. Amazingly, the bones possess all of these characteristics. A cube of bone 1 square inch in surface will bear, without being crushed, a weight of more than 4 tons. Ounce for ounce, bone is stronger than solid steel. And yet, a piece of bone will stretch 10 times as much as steel. A steel frame comparable to the human skeleton would weight 3 times as much. Alexander Macalister, former professor of anatomy at Cambridge University, has suggested: "Man's body is a machine formed for doing work. Its framework is the most suitable that could be devised in material, structure, and arrangement" (1886, 7:2).

As a specific example of bone design, consider the bones of the foot. One-fourth of all the body's bones are in the feet. Each human foot contains 26 bones. The feet have been designed to facilitate a number of mechanical functions. They **support**, using arches similar to those found in an engineered bridge. They operate as **levers** (as in those occasions when one presses an automobile accelerator peddle). They act like **hydraulic jacks** when a person tip-toes. They **catapult** a person as he jumps. And feet act as a **cushion** for the legs when one is running. All of these features are quite helpful—especially in view of the fact that an average person will walk about 65,000 miles in his/her lifetime (equivalent to traveling around the world more than two-and-a-half times). The skeletal system demonstrates brilliant design, to be sure. The conclusion is inescapable that there must have been a brilliant Designer behind it.

The Circulatory System

The circulatory system consists of the heart, blood, and blood vessels, and has several important functions. First, the circulatory system transports digested food particles to the various parts of the body. Second, it takes oxygen to the cells for burning food, thus producing heat and energy. Third, it picks up waste materials and carries them to the organs that eliminate wastes from the body as a whole.

The heart is a small muscle (or, as some would say, two muscles connected in tandem) in the upper chest cavity. Dr. Michael DeBakey has called it a "busy machine" that pumps blood to all part of the body (1984, 9:132a). In the adult male, the heart weighs about 11 ounces, and is about the size of a large fist; a woman's heart is slightly smaller. Miller and Goode have described this marvelous muscle as a "pump with a **built-in** motor" (1960, p. 63, emp. added). The question comes to mind: Is it not the case that something **built** always has a **builder**?

The heart is the strongest muscle in the body. Normally it beats (in an adult) at about 70 to 80 times per minute. When the body needs an extra supply of blood (e.g., during vigorous exercise), it can beat 150 to 180 times a minute—an automatic regulating feature that clearly indicates design. Note this unwitting testimony from an evolutionist.

> The heart and blood vessels do more than speed or slow our blood flow to meet [the body's] needs. They carry the scarlet stream to different tissues under differing pressures to fuel different actions. Blood rushes to the stomach when we eat, to the lungs and muscles when we swim, to the brain when we read. To satisfy these changing metabolic needs, the cardiovascular system **integrates information as well as any computer, then responds as no computer can** (Schiefelbein, 1986, p. 124, emp. added).

The force the heart exerts is tremendous. It can squirt a stream of blood about 10 feet into the air. In the span of a single hour, the heart generates enough energy to lift a medium-sized car 3 feet off the ground (Avraham, 1989, p. 13). The heart is an involuntary muscle that beats about 100,000 times a day, or nearly 40,000,000 times in a year. It pumps about 1,800 gallons of blood a day. In a lifetime, a heart will pump some 600,000 metric tons of blood!

What causes the heart to beat, however? It contains a small patch of tissue called the sinus node, or cardiac pacemaker. Somehow, about every 8/10 of a second, it produces an electrical current (a jump-start) to certain nerve fibers which stimulate the muscular contractions that send the blood flowing (at up to 10 miles per hour) throughout the body. The body's blood supply, which gets depleted of oxygen, is pumped back to the heart. From there it is conveyed to the lungs, where it is reoxygenated and sent once more to the various parts of the body. Blood, therefore, is being continuously pumped into, and out of, the heart with its rhythmic beating. Evolutionists Miller and Goode have conceded that "for a pump that is keeping two separate circulatory systems going in perfect synchronization, **it is hard to imagine a better job of engineering** (1960, p. 68, emp. added). Yet this amazing device, which they admit is "hard to describe as anything short of a **miracle**," allegedly was produced by blind forces in nature (1960, p. 64, emp. added). Medical authorities have observed that the heart's efficiency (i.e., the amount of useful work in relation to fuel expended) is about twice that of a steam engine (see Lenihan, 1974, p. 131). If intelligence was required to invent the steam engine, does it not stand to reason that intelligence lies behind the human heart?

Fifteen centuries before Christ was born, Moses declared that "the life of the flesh is in the blood" (Leviticus 17:11). This inspired truth was uttered more than 3,000 years before English physician William Harvey (1628) discovered the circulatory system. Actually, blood is classified as a tissue. The body contains about 5 to 6 quarts of this liquid tissue. The blood consists of plasma (which is mostly water), salts, a protein called fibrinogen, antibodies (which help fight disease), enzymes, and hormones. The plasma helps maintain chemical balance in the body, regulates the body's water content, and assists in controlling temperature. The blood also contains solid materials—red cells, white cells, and platelets. The 25 trillion red cells transport oxygen throughout the body, and carry carbon dioxide back to the lungs (via the heart). The white cells (5 different kinds) attack bacteria and other germs. They are the body's defensive army. The platelets (15 million in a single drop of blood) help the blood to clot when the body is wounded. They are the body's repairmen.

Harmful bacteria and worn-out cells are filtered out of the blood by the liver and the spleen. The kidneys also remove waste products from the blood system. The blood has a very effective garbage disposal system. Who could possibly believe that these wonderfully-integrated mechanisms simply happened by mere chance?

In order for blood to accomplish its vital work, it must remain at a relatively constant temperature. A radical drop in body temperature can damage the cells, and if the temperature rises above 108°F, one cannot survive for long. Amazingly, however, there is a thermostat in the brain that monitors the temperature of the blood as it flows through that organ. When the air temperature drops, the heart slows down and the blood vessels constrict, forcing the liquid tissue to flow deeper within the body where it can remain warm. When the weather gets warm, or when we exercise, the arterioles open and the blood is dispersed within the skin, effectively functioning like a radiator (see Schiefelbein, 1986, p. 128).

The blood vessels constitute an incredible pipeline system networking the entire body. These vessels come in three basic types: (1) arteries (and smaller arterioles) are vessels that carry blood away from the heart; (2) veins (and smaller venules) transport the blood back to the heart; and (3) capillaries are microscopic vessels that link the smallest arteries with veins. If all of the body's pipelines were connected end-to-end, it has been estimated that it would stretch to a length of between 60,000 and 100,000 miles. The system is "so efficient" that the entire process of circulation, "during which every cell in the body is serviced, takes only a total of 20 seconds" (Avraham, 1989, p. 41). Would any rational person deny that a major city's pipeline system was designed? Hardly. The body's skillfully-constructed transportation system clearly evinces design, hence a Designer. Lenihan confessed: "The circulation is an example of a multipurpose system, often found in the body but **generally beyond the capability of the engineering designer**" (1974, p. 5, emp. added).

In this connection, it might be noted that medical scientists, in the interest of extending human longevity, have attempted to fashion numerous artificial organs. All such efforts have met with only limited success. As one authority noted: "...no synthetic spare part—however well engineered—can match the capacity of the organ a normal human being is born with" (Mader, 1979, p. 367). Miller and Goode admitted that "no engineering genius has invented a pump like the human heart" (1960, p. 6). Dr. Pierre Galletti of Brown Medical School described artificial body parts as "simplistic substitutes for their sophisticated natural counterparts" (see Cauwels, 1986, p. ix). Man can attempt to duplicate the Grand Designer's handiwork, but he can never hope to approach the wisdom and skill of the Creator.

The arteries have been fashioned in such a way as to be both elastic and porous. The elasticity accommodates the surging blood, and also helps regulate body temperature. But how is the blood able to make its way, against gravity, back up the veins to the heart? The veins, it turns out, contain one-way valves with open ends that face the heart—analogous to the valves in an automobile engine (Miller and Goode, 1960, p. 71). The blood is pushed partially upward by force from the heart, but it also is propelled by muscle movements that massage the veins, pushing the blood forward through the valves. In the veins of the legs, these valves are spaced about every half inch.

The capillaries are the smallest yet most abundant of the blood vessels. It takes about 120 short capillaries to measure 3 inches. All of them laid end-to-end, however, would circle the equator twice (Avraham, 1989, p. 40). The blood is pumped into the capillaries with a force sufficient to drive the plasma and its rich cargo through the porous walls of these tiny vessels, thus renourishing the cells. This procedure requires a very "precise balance of pressures between the blood flowing within their walls and the fluid in and around the body's cells" (Schiefelbein, 1986, p. 114). Without question this delicately-balanced system affirms design. Some struggle to avoid such a conclusion, but at times they admit that:

If, like the scientists of an earlier day, we assumed a constant guiding purposefulness in our biological universe, we might say that the capillary system is the purpose of the circulation, that the entire system, heart and all, **was designed for just this end** (Miller and Goode, 1960, p. 77, emp. added).

The Nervous System

The nervous system is the "communication center" of the body, and consists of: (1) the **brain**; (2 the **spinal cord**; and (3) the **nerves**, which spread out from the brain and spinal cord to all parts of the body, somewhat like the root system of a tree. The nervous system has many functions. It regulates the actions of organs like the muscles, liver, kidneys, etc. It monitors the senses, such as seeing, hearing, feeling, etc. It also controls our thinking, learning, and memory capabilities.

The specialized nerve receptors in the sensory organs receive information from the environment. To chose just one example, in the skin their are some 3 to 4 million structures sensitive to pain. There are a half-million touch detectors and more than 200,000 temperature gauges. These tiny receptors, plus those in the eyes, ears, nose, tongue, etc., constantly send data to the brain. This information is transmitted (at up to 450 feet per second, or 30 miles per hour), via the nerve fibers to the brain. The transmission involves both electrical and chemical energy. The brain analyzes the data and determines the appropriate action to be taken. Noted science writer, John Pfeiffer, an evolutionist, has called the nervous system "the most elaborate communications system ever devised" (1961, p. 4). **Who** devised it? A number of years ago, the prestigious journal, *Natural History*, contained this statement: "The nervous system of a single starfish, with all its various nerve ganglia and fibers, is more complex than London's telephone exchange" (Burnett, 1961, p. 17). If that is true for the nervous system of the lowly starfish, what could be said about the infinitely more complex nervous system of the human?

The brain, located in the protective case called the skull, is the most highly-specialized organ in the body. The late Isaac Asimov, well-known science writer and humanist, once stated that man's brain is "the most complex and orderly arrangement of matter in the universe" (1970, p. 10). **Who** arranged it? Paul Davies, atheistic professor of mathematics and physics at the Universe of Adelaide, observed that the human brain is "the most developed and complex system known to science" (1992, 14[5]:4).

The human brain, which weighs about three pounds, consists of three main areas. The cerebrum is the thinking/learning center. It deciphers messages from the sensory organs and controls the voluntary muscles. Evolutionist William Beck spoke of the "architectural plan" characteristic of this region (1971, p. 444). Does not an "architectural plan" require an architect? The maintenance of equilibrium and muscle coordination occurs in the cerebellum. Finally, there is the brain stem, which has several components that control the involuntary muscles—regulating heartbeat, digestion, breathing, etc.

Let us consider several aspects of the brain's uncanny abilities. [Incidentally, human beings, unlike animals, are the only creatures who think about their brains!] The brain's memory storage capacity is incredible. It has been compared to a vast library. Evolutionist Carl Sagan of Cornell University has written:

> The information content of the human brain expressed in bits is probably comparable to the total number of connections among the neurons—about a hundred trillion, 10^{14} bits. If written out in English, say, that information would fill some twenty million volumes, as many as in the world's largest libraries. The equivalent of twenty million books is inside the heads of every one of us. The brain is a very big place in a very small space (1979, p. 275).

It has been suggested that it would take a bookshelf 500 miles long—from San Francisco, California to Portland, Oregon—to house the information stored in the human brain. Would anyone actually contend that this kind of information content "just happened"? Evolutionists do. A popular science journal employed this analogy.

> The brain is an immense computer with 1^{10} circuits and a memory of perhaps 10^{20} bits, each of these being five to ten orders of magnitude more complex than any computer yet built. It is still more fascinating that the brain performs this work, using only 20 to 25 watts compared to the six and ten kilowatts used by our large computers (Cahill, 1981, 89[3]:105).

One writer has suggested that "many researchers think of the brain as a computer. This comparison is inadequate. Even the most sophisticated computers that we can envision are crude compared to the almost infinite complexity and flexibility of the human brain" (Pines, 1986, p. 326). The Cray-2 supercomputer has a storage capacity about 1,000 times less than that of a human brain. One authority stated that "problem solving by a human brain exceeds by far the capacity of the most powerful computers" (*Encyclopaedia Britannica*, 1989, 2:189).

No rational person subscribes to the notion that the computer "just happened by chance" as the result of fortuitous accidents in nature. The computer obviously was designed, and that demands a designer. Nobel laureate Sir John Eccles, an evolutionist, conceded the design evinced by the brain's amazing memory capacity when he wrote:

> We do not even begin to comprehend the functional significance of this richly complex **design**.... If we now persist in regarding the brain as a machine, then we must say that it is by far the most complicated machine in existence (1958, pp. 135,136, emp. added).

If the less-complicated computer indicates design, what does this say for the infinitely more complex human brain? Evolutionist Richard Dawkins has argued that the Universe is without design. In spite of that, however, he wrote:

> The brain with which you are understanding my words is an array of some ten million kiloneurons. Many of these billions of nerve cells have each more than a thousand "electric wires" connecting them to other neurons. Moreover, at the molecular genetic level, every single one of more than a trillion cells in the body contains about a thousand times as much precisely-coded digital information as my entire computer. The complexity of living organisms is matched by the elegant efficiency of their apparent design. If anyone doesn't agree that this amount of complex design cries out for an explanation, I give up (1986, p. ix)

In addition to its phenomenal memory capacity, the brain also exhibits extraordinary ability in its orchestration of muscular movements. Suppose you decide that you want to pick up a pen and some paper from your desk. Your brain will have to send signals to your hands, wrists, arms, and shoulders, which will direct the manipulation of 60 different joints and more than 100 muscles. In addition to moving the muscles directionally, the brain regulates the exact force needed for a particular task. Opening the car door of your classic 1937 Chevrolet requires 400 times more torque (turning force) than dialing a rotary-style telephone. Picking up a paper clip requires only a fraction of an ounce of force, whereas pulling on your socks and shoes necessitates about 8 to 12 pounds of force. The brain compensates for multiplied thousands of these kinds of variables in daily life. Too, it does its work efficiently in terms of energy use. One scientist observed that "half a salted peanut provides sufficient calories for an hour of intense mental effort" (Pfeiffer, 1961, p. 102). Evolutionist Robert Jastrow concluded:

> The average human brain weighs three pounds, consumes electrical energy at the rate of 25 watts, and occupies a volume of one-tenth of a cubic foot. ...a machine matching the human brain in memory capacity would consume electrical energy at the rate of one billion watts—half the output of the Grand Coulee Dam—and occupy most of the space of the Empire State

Building. Its cost would be in the neighborhood of $10 billion. The machine would be a prodigious artificial intelligence, but it would be only a clumsy imitation of the human brain (1981, pp. 142,143).

One of the astounding features of the brain is its ability to process and react to so many different circumstances at once. While an artist is working on a painting (using his voluntary muscles at the behest of this brain), he can: smell food cooking and know whether it is turnip greens or steak; hear a dog barking and determine if it is his dog or a neighbor's; feel a breeze upon his face and sense that rain is near; and be reflecting on a warm friendship of the past. Even while all of this is taking place, the brain is regulating millions of internal bodily activities that the person never even "thinks" about.

Logical contemplation of these facts can only lead one to agree with prominent brain surgeon, Robert White, who wrote: "I am left with no choice but to acknowledge the existence of a Superior Intellect, responsible for the design and development of the incredible brain-mind relationship—something far beyond man's capacity to understand" (1978, p. 99). Jastrow himself even admitted: "It is not so easy to accept that theory [Darwin's theory of evolution by natural selection—BT/WJ] as the explanation of an extraordinary organ like the brain" (1981, p. 96). Dr. Jastrow went on to say: "Among the organs of the human body, none is more difficult that the brain to explain by evolution" (1981, p. 104).

And it is not just the brain that is "difficult to explain by evolution." Were space to permit, we could examine numerous other body systems (e.g., digestive, reproductive, etc.), each of which provides clear and compelling evidence of design. Atheistic philosopher Paul Ricci has suggested that "Although many have difficulty understanding the tremendous **order and complexity** of functions of the human body (the eye, for example), **there is no obvious designer**" (1986, p. 191, emp. added). The only people who "have difficulty understanding the tremendous order and complexity" found in the Universe are those who have "refused to have God in their knowledge" (Romans 1:28). Such people can parrot the phrase that "there is no obvious designer," but their arguments are not convincing in light of the evidence at hand.

The Unbeliever's Response to the Argument from Design

In the past, those who chose not to believe in God denied the existence of any purposeful design in the Universe, and busied themselves in attempting to prove that point. That is why, for example, Richard Dawkins wrote *The Blind Watchmaker*—to argue that there is **no design** apparent in the Universe. Were such design found to exist, the conclusion would be both inescapable and undeniable—there must have been a designer.

It is not an easy task, however, to explain away what the average person can see so readily as evidence of design. There are simply too many striking examples of design in nature, which is teeming with creatures, and features, that can be explained only by an appeal to an intelligent designer. From the macrocosm to the microcosm, inherent design is clearly evident. In their more lucid moments, event unbelievers are struck by it. Evolutionist Douglas Futuyma, for example, ruefully admitted: "We look at the design of organisms, then, for evidence of the Creator's intelligence, and what do we see? A multitude of exquisite adaptations to be sure; the bones of a swallow beautifully adapted for flight; the eyes of a cat magnificently shaped for seeing in the twilight" (1983, p. 198).

Does this mean, then, that unbelievers like Dr. Futuyma have admitted defeat, and now are willing to accept the existence of God? Hardly. Rather than admit the existence of the Creator, they have developed a two-pronged approach to dealing with the theist's argument from design. First, they have developed an argument which suggests that apparent design is just that—apparent, not actual. In other words, features that

- 49 -

appear to have been designed can, in actuality, be explained on the basis of adaptation, random chance operating over eons of time, etc.

Second, they have developed an argument intended to draw attention away from apparent design in nature, and to call attention to alleged examples of "non-design" or poor design—which they feel should not be present if an intelligent Designer created the magnificent Universe in which we live. This line of reasoning basically suggests that if design in the Universe **proves** the existence of God, then "non-design" (or poor design) just as emphatically **disproves** the existence of that same God. In logical form, the argument may be stated as follows.

1. If the Universe evinces traits of non-design, there is no Designer.
2. The Universe does evince non-design.
3. Thus, the Universe had no Designer.

In recent years, this argument has grown in popularity. Dr. Futuyma, in his book, *Science on Trial*, devoted almost an entire chapter to examples of non-design in nature. Other scientists have joined in the fracas as well, not the least of whom is Harvard scientist Stephen Jay Gould, who has written extensively about alleged examples of non-design in nature.

As a result of all the attention being given to the matter of design versus non-design, a new phrase has been coined to express the unbeliever's position—the **argument from suboptimality**. This idea suggests that if all design were considered perfect, everything would be **optimal**; however, since there are items in nature that (allegedly) are imperfect, there is **suboptimality** in nature. [NOTE: The argument also is known as the argument from dysteleology.] It is our contention that the argument is flawed for several reasons.

First, in arguing the case for design, creationists are not obligated to show **obvious** design in every single feature of the Universe. It is necessary to produce only a reasonable number of sufficient evidences in order to establish design. **For the evolutionist to produce an example of something which, to him, evinces either non-design, or poor design, does not somehow magically negate all the other evidences of obvious design!**

Second, it is possible that an object possesses purposeful design, but that it is not recognized by the observer. Consider the following two cases. Percival Davis, in the book he co-authored with Wayne Frair, *A Case for Creation*, provided the following illustration.

> My daughter was playing with her pet rat one day when a question occurred to her. "Daddy," she said, "why does a rat have scales on its tail?"
>
> "You know perfectly well," I replied. "The reptiles that were ancestral to rats and all other mammals had scales on their tails as well as on the rest of their bodies. Because there was no particular disadvantage to having them, they persisted in rats to this day."
>
> "Quit putting me on, Daddy. I know you don't believe that!"
>
> You cannot win, it seems. But it is true that one is hard put to discern the reason for the manifold adaptations that organisms possess. What I should have said to my daughter (and eventually did say) was that God had put the scales there for reasons He knew to be perfectly good ones but which may take us a lot of research to discover, since He has not told us what they are. Still, the fact was that I could not explain the presence of those scales... (Frair and Davis, 1983, pp. 30-31).

Dr. Davis has raised two very important points with this simple story. First, we may not know **presently** why an organism is designed the way it is. To us, the design is either not yet recognizable, or not yet well understood. Second, with further research, the heretofore unrecognizable design eventually may be discovered. In fact, in the case which follows, that is exactly what happened.

- 51 -

In his book, *The Panda's Thumb*, Dr. Gould (one of suboptimality's most vocal supporters) presented what he believed to be perhaps the finest known example of non-design to be found in nature thus far—the panda's thumb. After providing an exhaustive explanation of how the panda has 5 other digits on each "hand," which function quite well in the panda's everyday life, Dr. Gould then provided an equally exhaustive explanation of the panda's "thumb." It is, he said, "a somewhat clumsy, but quite workable" appendage that "wins no prize in an engineer's derby." His whole essay was intended to portray this as good evidence of suboptimality—i.e., non-design in nature. In fact, lest the reader miss his point, Gould said that "odd arrangements and funny solutions are the proof of evolution—paths that a sensible God would never tread, but that a natural process, constrained by history, follows perforce" (1980, pp. 20-21).

Interestingly, while Dr. Gould was writing about the non-design that he felt was so evident, research (the same kind of research Dr. Davis suggested was needed to elucidate the purpose of design in certain structures) was ongoing in regard to the panda's thumb. What did that research show? The panda's thumb has now been found to exhibit design for very special functions, as the following information attests.

First, the San Diego Zoo's *Giant Panda Zoobook* states: "In fact, the giant panda is one of the few large animals that can grab things as tightly as a human can" (undated, p. 6). Second, in 1985 Schaller and co-authors released *The Giant Pandas of Wolong*, in which they wrote: "The panda can handle bamboo stems with great precision by holding them as if with forceps in the hairless groove connecting the pad of the first digit and pseudothumb" (p. 4).

Do these kinds of statements seem to describe the panda's thumb as a "jury-rigged" device? Does being able to grasp something tightly, with great precision, using a pseudothumb that can be compared to surgical forceps seem to convey non-design? Such statements should serve to remind us that an object may indeed possess purposeful design, but that design may not be evident immediately to the observer. Dr. Gould could not see (for whatever reasons) the design in the panda's thumb. Nevertheless, such design is present.

There are other flaws with the suboptimality argument as well. One of the most serious is this: **those who claim that something is "suboptimal" must, by definition, set themselves up as the sole judge of what is, and what is not, "optimal."** In other words, those who would claim non-design in nature must know two things: (1) they must know with certainty that the item under discussion positively evinces no design; and (2) they must know with certainty what the absolute standard is in the first place (i.e., "the optimal") in order to claim that something has become "suboptimal."

These points have not escaped evolutionary scientists. For example, S.R. Scadding of Guelph University in Canada has commented that the suboptimality "argument is a theological rather than a scientific argument, since it is based on the **supposed** nature of the Creator" (1981, p. 174, emp. added). That is to say, the unbeliever sets himself up as the Creator, presupposes to know the mind of the Creator, and then presumes to say what the Creator did, or did not, do. Observe how one evolutionist does just that:

> The case for evolution then has two sides; positive evidence—that evolution has occurred; and negative evidence—that the natural world does not conform to **our expectation** of what an omnipotent, omniscient, truthful Creator **would have** created (Futuyma, 1983, p. 198, emp. added).

Notice the phrase, "that the natural world does not conform to **our expectation** of what an omnipotent, omniscient, truthful Creator **would have** created." The atheist, agnostic, or skeptic looks at the creation, sees that it does not fit what **he** would do if **he** were the Creator, and then suggests on that basis that a Creator does not exist. Such thinking makes for an extremely weak argument. As Frair and Davis have remarked: "It could be considered arrogant to assume knowledge of a design feature's purpose in an organism, even if it had a purpose" (1983, p. 31).

There is yet another flaw in this suboptimality argument, which, like the one just discussed, has to do with theology, not science. First, the unbeliever sets himself up as the Creator, and proceeds to note that since things weren't done as he would do them, there must not be a Creator. Second, however, when the **real** Creator tries to explain why things are as they are, the unbeliever refuses to listen. We offer the following in support of this point.

It is at least possible that an object once clearly reflected purposeful design, but as a result of a process of degeneration, the design has been clouded or erased. Suppose a gardener, digging in a pile of rubbish, discovers an ancient book. Its cover is weathered, its pages are mostly stuck together, the type has faded, etc. It is, for all practical purposes, completely illegible. Does the **current** condition of the book mean that it never had a message—that it never evidenced design? Of course not. Though the book is in a degenerative condition, and the message has faded with time, there is no denying that the book was at one point quite communicative.

The unbeliever surveys the Earth and finds examples of what he believes are evidences of "suboptimality." Yet in many cases he may be witnessing simply degeneration instead. In fact, that is exactly what the Creator has stated. When man sinned, and evil was introduced to this planet, a state of progressive degeneration commenced. The whole creation suffered as a result of man's sin (Romans 8:20-22). The Hebrew writer, quoting the psalmist, observed that "the earth, like a garment, is wearing out (Hebrews 1:10-11).

This important point also should be noted: the fact that the product of an orderly mechanism is flawed does not necessarily reflect upon either the initial design or the designer. For example, if a machine that manufactures tin cans begins to turn out irregular cans, does this somehow prove the machine had no designer? Must one postulate that the machine's inventor intended for mutilated cans to be produced, or that the machine was imperfectly designed? Surely we can conceive that the failure could be on the part of those who failed to follow the correct procedures for maintaining the machine, or who abused it in some fashion.

When man rebelled against his Maker, the Lord allowed, as a consequence of that disobedience, degenerative processes to begin, which eventually result in death (Romans 5:12). But the fact that we have eye problems, heart failure, diseases, etc., does not negate the impact as a whole that the human body is "fearfully and wonderfully made" (Psalm 139:14). We will not assume, therefore, that because an unbeliever's reasoning ability is flawed, this proves his brain was not designed. The design argument remains unscathed.

Unbelievers, of course, ignore all this. After all, they have already set themselves up as the Creator, and have determined that none of this is the way they would do it. When the real Creator speaks, they are too busy playing the Creator to hear Him. Futuyma has written:

> The creationists admit that species can undergo limited adaptive changes by the mechanism of mutation plus natural selection. But surely an omniscient and omnipotent Creator could devise a more foolproof method than random mutation to enable his creatures to adapt. Yet mutations do occur, and we have experimental demonstration that they are not oriented in the direction of better adaptedness. How could a wise Creator, in fact, allow mutations to happen at all, since they are so often degenerative instead of uplifting? According to the creationists, there is "a basic principle of disintegration now at work in nature" that we must suppose includes mutation. But why should the Creator have established such a principle? Didn't He like the perfection of His original creation (1983, p. 200)?

Dr. Futuyma acknowledges that creationists have tried to get him to see that there is "a basic principle of disintegration now at work in nature." Then he asks, "But why should the Creator have established such a principle? Didn't He like the perfection of His original creation?" This is why we say that the problem is rooted in theology, not science. Futuyma questions why the Creator enacted this "principle of degeneration," then makes it clear that he has no intention whatsoever of accepting the answer provided by the very Creator he questions. If Dr. Futuyma had studied what the Creator did say, he would have the answer to his question. Yes, the Creator liked His original creation, so much so He pronounced it "very good" (Genesis 1:31).

It was not God's fault that the principle of degeneration became a reality. It was man's fault because the first man wanted, like so many today, to be his own God. Is there a "principle of degeneration" at work? Indeed there is. Might it cause some organisms or structures to have their original message (i.e., design) diminished, or to lose it altogether? Certainly. But does that mean that there never was any design? Or, does it reflect poorly on the Designer, proving somehow that He does not exist? In the eyes of the unbeliever, the only possible answer to these questions is a resounding "yes." As Scadding has noted:

> Haeckel makes clear why this line of argument was of such importance to early evolutionary biologists.... It seemed difficult to explain functionless structures on the basis of special creation without imputing some lack of skill in design to the Creator (1981, p. 174).

So, God gets the blame for man's mistakes. And, the unbeliever get another argument for his arsenal. Here, in a nutshell, is that argument, as stated by British evolutionist Jeremy Cherfas:

> In fact, as Darwin recognized, a perfect Creator could manufacture perfect adaptations. Everything would fit because everything was designed to fit. It is in the imperfect adaptations that natural selection is revealed,

because it is those imperfections that show us that structure has a history. If there were no imperfections, there would be no evidence of history, and therefore nothing to favor evolution by natural selection over creation (1984, p. 29).

Henry Morris, speaking specifically about the comments made by Cherfas, has made an interesting observation:

> This is an amazing admission. The main evidence against creation and for evolution is that natural selection doesn't work! If there were no "imperfect" structures in nature, the evidence would all favor creation. No wonder evolution has to be imposed by authority and bombast, rather than reason, if this is its only real evidence! (1985, p. 177).

Yet this is exactly what Gould has suggested: "Odd arrangements and funny solutions are the **proof of evolution...**" (1980, p. 20, emp. added).

The theist, however, is not willing to usurp the Creator's prerogative and, like the unbeliever, tell Him what He can (and cannot) do, or what is (and what is not) acceptable. As Frair and Davis have suggested:

> Yet the creationist lacks the option (open to the evolutionist) of assuming **purposelessness**. Human curiosity being what it is, the creationist will be motivated to inquire concerning the purpose of the universe and all its features. The purpose for most things will not be found. What we do find may, nonetheless, be sufficient justification for the endeavor (1983, pp. 31-32, emp. in orig.).

It is clear that unbelievers are grasping at straws when the argument from suboptimality is the best they can offer. In reality, of course, all of this is nothing new. Darwin, in his *Origin of Species*, addressed essentially the same argument in 1859. Modern unbelievers—desperate to find something they can use as evidence against design in the Universe (and thus against the Designer)—have resurrected it from the relic heaps of history, dusted it off, given it a different name, and attempted to imbue it with respectability while foisting it upon the public as a legitimate response to the argument from design. Once again they have had to set themselves up as the Creator in order to try to convince people that no Creator exists. And, once again, they have failed. One does not get a poem without a poet, or a law without a lawgiver. One does not get a painting without a painter, or a musical score without a composer. And just as surely, one does not get purposeful design without a designer. The design inherent within the Universe—from the macrocosm to the microcosm—is quite evident, and is sufficient to draw the conclusion demanded by the evidence, in keeping with the law of rationality, that God does exist.

4
Morality and Ethics—
The Anthropological Argument

All rational people are concerned, to a greater or lesser degree, about human moral and ethical conduct. How we act, and are acted upon, with respect to our fellow man determines the progress and happiness of mankind and, ultimately, contributes in one form or another to human destiny. The existence of, and need for, morality and ethics are self-evident. No sane person would argue that absolutely anything goes. The expressions "ought" and "ought not" are as much a part of the atheist's vocabulary as anyone else's. While it is true that a person may become so insensitive that he abandons virtually all of his personal ethical obligations, he will never be willing to ignore the lack of such in those who would abuse him.

So far as creatures of the Earth are concerned, morality is uniquely a human trait—a fact even unbelievers concede. For example, although evolutionist George Gaylord Simpson argued that "man is the result of a purposeless and materialistic process that did not have him in mind," he admitted that "good and evil, right and wrong, concepts irrelevant in nature except from the human viewpoint, become real and pressing fea tures of the whole cosmos as viewed morally because **morals arise only in man**" (1951, p. 179, emp. added). Animals do not operate according to any ethical code. A dog feels no pangs of conscience when it steals a bone from its peers; a cock knows no remorse when mortally wounding another. Men, however, acknowledge the existence of morality and ethics.

Since it is evident universally that morals and ethics do exist, the question becomes: What is their origin? There are but two options. Morality and ethics are either: **theocentric**—that is, centered in an external source of eternal goodness, namely, God; or **anthropocentric**—that is, grounded in the mind of man as a creature that evolved naturally as a result of inanimate forces operating over eons of cosmic and geologic time (see Geisler and Corduan, 1988, pp. 109-122).

How does atheism explain the origin of morality? Since the unbeliever does not believe that there is an eternal Mind with which goodness is coexistent, i.e., an intrinsically moral Being, obviously he must contend that somehow raw, eternal, inorganic matter was able, by means of an extended evolutionary process, to concoct, promote, and maintain morality. Such a theory is self-defeating for two reasons. First, it wrongly assumes that man, with that evolved mass of cerebral tissue between his ears, somehow is capable of discovering "moral truth." Why should he be? Charles Darwin declared that "there is no fundamental difference between man and the higher mammals in their mental faculties" (as quoted in Francis Darwin, 1889, 1:64). Since no other animal on the long, meandering evolutionary chain can locate and live by "moral truth," should we then be expected to trust a "naked ape" (to use evolutionary zoologist Desmond Morris' colorful expression) to formulate ethics? Darwin himself opined: "Can the mind of man, which has, as I fully believe, been developed from a mind as low as that possessed by the lowest animals, be trusted when it draws such grand conclusions?" (as quoted in Francis Darwin, 1889, 1:282).

Second, it should be clear that "raw matter" is impotent to evolve any sense of moral consciousness. Simpson inadvertently conceded this point when he wrote:

> Discovery that the universe apart from man or before his coming lacks and lacked any purpose or plan has the inevitable corollary that the workings of the universe cannot provide any automatic, universal, eternal, or absolute ethical criteria of right and wrong (1951, p. 180).

Unbelief therefore must, and does, contend that there is no ultimate standard of moral/ethical truth, and that morality and ethics are, at best, relative and situational. Thus, if morality is man-authorized, hence, man-centered, it is utterly impossible to argue for any singular system of ethics to which one could consistently urge his fellows to subscribe. Rather, billions of ethical systems would exist (as many as there are people), each frequently at variance with many of the others, yet, oddly, each equally valid. Who could ever charge correctly that someone else's conduct was "wrong," or that a man "ought" or "ought not" to do thus and so? The simple fact of the matter is that infidelity cannot reasonably explain the origin of morality and ethics. These concepts can be explained adequately only by appealing to the existence of an omnipotent, omniscient God.

An examination into the existence of morality and ethics provides yet another link in the chain of logical thought that establishes the case for the existence of God. The evidence is often discussed by means of what is referred to as the anthropological, or moral, argument for God's existence. Morality is the character of being in accord with the principles or standards of right conduct. Ethics is generally viewed as the system or code by which attitudes and actions are determined to be either right or wrong. Ethics is sometimes defined as the justification of criteria by which one human life can be judged to be better or worse than another (see Henry, 1973, p. 220). Morality and ethics, then, assert that there exists a differentiation between right and wrong, and between good and evil. Moreover, by implication, there must be an appeal to some ultimate standard by which these character traits can be distinguished. The purpose of morality and ethics is inseparably connected with the purpose of life itself.

If there is no purpose in the Universe, as Simpson and others have asserted, then actually there is no purpose to morality or ethics. But the concept of a purposeless morality, or a purposeless ethic, does not make sense, and so men have sought to read some meaning, as far-fetched as it may be, into the natural human inclination to recognize the need for morality. Let us give brief attention to several of the theories that propose to explain the function of human ethics.

Hedonism

Hedonism is the philosophy which argues that the aim of moral conduct is the attainment of the greatest possible pleasure with the greatest possible avoidance of pain. That is to say, the single moral criterion is the preponderance of pleasure over pain. A phase of hedonism, known as psychological hedonism, contends that one can act **only** in this manner. But if that is the case, how could one's actions be considered as "moral" in such circumstances? A man can hardly be viewed as moral for doing that which he cannot help doing.

Hedonism, however, is woefully inconsistent, and its advocates will rarely, if ever, stay with its logical conclusions. What if one, in the pursuit of pleasure and the avoidance of pain, must inflict pain upon others in order to achieve the goal? In other words, what if one must act **immorally** in order to practice his "morality"? What is there about hedonism that would motivate a person to forego his own pleasure in the interest of others? Absolutely nothing! Renowned British agnostic Bertrand Russell frustratingly wrote:

> We feel that the man who brings widespread happiness at the expense of misery to himself is a better man than the man who brings unhappiness to others and happiness to himself. I do not know of any rational ground for this view, or, perhaps, for the somewhat more rational view

that whatever the majority desires [called utilitarian hedonism—BT/WJ] is preferable to what the minority desires. These are truly ethical problems but I do not know of any way in which they can be solved except by politics or war. All that I can find to say on this subject is that **an ethical opinion can only be defended by an ethical axiom, but, if the axiom is not accepted, there is no way of reaching a rational conclusion** (1969, 3:29, emp. added).

But what if a person is simply an egotistical hedonist and thus announces, "I care not at all for others; I intend to live my life solely for my own pleasure with no consideration for others, save when such is in my own interest." But someone doubtlessly would be tempted to respond, "That is so selfish." So, what is wrong with selfishness if it brings pleasure to the committed hedonist? Some are willing to actually go to that extreme. Atheistic philosopher Ayn Rand even authored a book titled, *The Virtue of Selfishness—A New Concept of Egoism*, defending the concept of hedonistic selfishness. Yet who would want to live in such a society?

Utilitarianism

Utilitarianism, advocated by Jeremy Bentham, J.S. Mill, and others, is built upon the foundation of hedonism, and argues that "good" is that which gives pleasure to the greatest number of people. Again, however, the theory is seriously flawed for several reasons. First, it cannot answer the vital query: If pleasure to the greatest number of people prevents a man from achieving his own personal pleasure, what is there to motivate him toward the pleasure of the many? Second, utilitarianism provides no guideline to determine what the "pleasure" (genuine happiness) of the many actually is. Third, it is the philosophy that stands behind, and is perfectly consistent with, numerous atrocities perpetrated in the alleged interest of humanity. When Hitler slaughtered countless millions, and bred people like animals to evolve his "master race," he felt he was operating in the genuine interest of mankind as a whole. The principle is: If some have to suffer in order for the ultimate good to be accomplished, so what? Of course, the leaders of such movements are always willing to step forward with their definition of what that "ultimate good" is!

Finally, however, this idea cannot provide any rational reason as to why it would be "wrong" to ignore what is in the interest of the many and, instead, simply pursue one's personal pleasure. There is an amazing commentary on this point in the book, *My Father Bertrand Russell*, written by Russell's daughter, Katherine Tait. Mrs. Tait was born in London in 1923, and was educated at her parents' innovative school, Beacon Hill, which was dedicated to the promotion of atheistic humanism. In her fascinating volume, Mrs. Tait explained what it was like being the famous philosopher's only daughter.

For example, Bertrand Russell believed that a parent must teach his child "with its very first breath that it has entered into a moral world" (Tait, 1975, p. 59). Yet, as with all atheists and agnostics, he had a most difficult time explaining why, if man is merely the product of natural forces, children should be taught morality. Tait recalled that as a child she might say, in connection with some moral responsibility, "I don't want to! Why should I?" A conventional parent, she observed, might reply, "Because I say so..., your father says so..., God says so...." Russell, however, would say to his children: "Because more people will be happy if you do than if you don't." "So what," she would respond, "I don't care about other people." But her father would declare, "You should!" In her naive innocence, young Katherine would inquire, "But why?"—a question to which the redundant rejoinder would be, "Because more people will be happy if you do than if you don't." And, Tait noted, "We felt the heavy pressure of his rectitude and obeyed, but the reason was not convincing—neither to us nor to him" (1975, pp. 184-185). Indeed, such specious reasoning will convince no one who thinks beyond the superficial level.

Morals/Ethics and the Existence of God

The truth of the matter is that only the theocentric approach to morality can explain the purpose of life, and therefore provide adequate motivation for a genuinely ethical approach to life. Though proof of God's existence is abundantly evident in the beautifully-designed Universe, His character is made known only in His verbal communications (available to us in the biblical documents). Thus, the Bible declares that God is eternal (Psalm 90:2; I Timothy 1:17), and that He is morally perfect. Not only is God holy (Isaiah 6:3; Revelation 4:8), just and righteous (Psalm 89:14), and good (Psalms 100:6; 106:1), but in the ultimate sense, **only** God is good (Mark 10:18). Since the God of the Bible is perfect (Matthew 5:48), it is to be expected that all that proceeds from Him is good initially. Accordingly, that which He created was good (Genesis 1:31), and all that He does, commands, and approves is likewise good (Psalm 119:39,68).

The "good," therefore, is what God is; what He has commanded results from Who He is, and thus is likewise good. In the Old Testament, the prophet Micah declared of God: "He showed thee, O man, what is good; and what doth Jehovah require of thee, but to do justly, and to love kindness, and walk humbly with thy God" (Micah 6:8). Similarly, in the New Testament Peter admonished: "...as he who called you is holy, be ye yourselves also holy in all manner of living; because it is written, Ye shall be holy: for I am holy" (I Peter 1:15).

Moral sensitivity (i.e., the awareness that right and wrong do exist) has been implanted in the soul of man by virtue of his creation in the image of the God Who is eternally good. Though created upright, man, as a being of free willpower, fell from his lofty estate. Accordingly, God, by means of divine revelation, seeks to bring man back into harmony with Himself—a process that entails both religious and moral obligations.

Biblical morality has several thrusts: (1) It is designed to develop within man right attitudes, or to state it another way, to instill a divine level of thinking; (2) Too, it is intended to help humanity translate spiritual attitudes into actions that will be helpful to all others; (3) Finally, the desired result is to guide man back into accord with the divine ideal, ensuring both his present and eternal happiness—to the glory of God.

Additionally, we may note that biblical revelation provides a sufficient motive for moral conduct. Those who have not foolishly thrust God from their minds (Psalm 14:1) acknowledge that the creation testifies of Jehovah's existence (Romans 1:20-21), and that His orderly Universe is evidence of His good and loving nature (Acts 14:17; James 1:17; I John 4:8). The love of God in providing Christ (John 3:16) for sinful man, and the love of Jesus in offering Himself to redeem us (Revelation 1:5; Philippians 2:5ff.), are motive aplenty for leading a moral life. We love, hence, obey Him (John 14:15) because He first loved us (I John 4:10-11,19). The Scriptures provide both **purpose** and **motive** for their ethical base, whereas unbelief provides neither.

Other Criteria for Establishing Ethics

All theories regarding morality assume some standard by which moral judgments are made. Whether that standard is "pleasure," "majority opinion," "survival," etc., these theories all have one thing in common: they assume some sort of ethical "yardstick" by which conduct is measured. We shall now give brief attention to several of these proposed standards to see how they fare in the light of logical scrutiny.

Nihilism

Nihilism springs from the atheistic notion that since there is no God, there can be no rational justification for ethical norms. Advocates of this viewpoint have contended that nihilism is the condition which allows that "everything is permitted." Russian novelist Fedor Dostoevski, in his work, *The Brothers Karamazov* (1880), has one of his characters say that if God is dead, **everything** is allowed. French existential philosopher, Jean Paul Sartre, wrote:

> Everything is indeed permitted if God does not exist, and man is in consequence forlorn, for he cannot find anything to depend upon either within or outside himself.... Nor, on the other hand, if God does not exist, are we provided with any values or commands that could legitimize our behavior (1961, p. 485).

Sartre contended that **whatever** one chooses to do is right; value is attached to the choice itself so that "...we can never choose evil" (1966, p. 279). These men are correct about one thing. If there is no God, "anything goes." The hypocrisy of this dogma, however, is revealed by the fact that the propagators of such an idea really mean that "everything is permitted" **for them alone**. They do not mean that the theft of **their** property, the rape of **their** wives, and the slitting of **their** throats is permitted!

Relativism

Moral relativism rejects the idea that there can be universal criteria for determining values. All value systems are thought to be culturally-originated and conditioned, hence, all cultural ethical systems are equally valid. No moral system, it is claimed, can be said to be either true or false.

Again, though, relativism falls of its own weaknesses, and its proponents will not stay with it. What if a particular culture, e.g., that of the "Bible Belt," believes that ethics is absolute? Would the relativists yield to that? Hardly! In some cultures, infanticide has been (or is being) deemed a proper form of population control. Is that then "right"? What about slavery, or the abuse of women? Where is the relativist that will declare openly and publicly the morality of such practices?

Situationism

Situationism (commonly known as "situation ethics") also repudiates the concept of any absolute system of values. For our present purpose, we may divide situationists into two classes—atheists and theists.

The atheistic position perhaps is best expressed in the *Humanist Manifestos I and II*. Written in 1933 and 1973, respectively, and signed by such notables as John Dewey, Isaac Asimov, Francis Crick, Julian Huxley, Antony Flew, and others, they contain the following statements:

> We affirm that moral values derive their source from human experience. Ethics is autonomous, and situational, needing no theological or ideological sanction. Ethics stems from human needs and interests. To deny this distorts the whole basis of life (*Humanist Manifestos I and II*, 1977, p. 17).

A more contradictory and absurd position would be difficult to conceive. If one argues that ethics is **situational**, he is suggesting that an act cannot be judged by an absolute standard, and that its rightness or wrongness is dependent upon the situation. For example, it would be wrong to lie if that falsehood was hurtful to others; however, if the lie could be helpful, it is said, then it would be right. However, as previously indicated, morality is alleged to be **autonomous**. That word means "self law," suggesting that every man is his own law. If that is the case, how could there ever be a situation in which a person could do wrong? Human ethical autonomy and situational morality are mutually exclusive.

Then there is theistic situation ethics, most popularly expounded by Joseph Fletcher. Fletcher (1966, p. 55) claimed that situation ethics represents a sort of the middle-of-the-road position between the extremes of "antinomianism" (i.e., no ethical rules exist) and "legalism" (i.e., moral decisions may be made by appealing to a rule book, e.g., the Bible). For him, "love" was the sole factor in making moral judgments. It must be noted, though, that his "love" is purely subjective—each individual must decide for himself, in a given context, what the "loving course" is.

The theory is fraught with insuperable logical difficulties. First, it affirms, "There are absolutely no absolutes." "Are you sure," we would ask? "Absolutely!" claims the situationist. Situation ethics claims there are no rules save the rule to love, yet by their own rules the situationists would define love. Second, God is removed from the throne as the moral Sovereign of the Universe, and man is enthroned in His place. Man, then, with his own subjective sense of "love," makes all final moral judgments. Situationism thus ignores the biblical view that man is lacking in sufficient wisdom to guide his earthly activities (Jeremiah 10:23). Third, Fletcher's situationism assumes a sort of omniscience in the application of his "love" principle. For example, the theory contends that lying, adultery, murder, etc., could be "moral" if done within the context of love. Yet, who is able to predict the consequences of such acts and determine, in advance, what is the "loving" thing to do? Let us suggest the following case.

A young woman, jilted by her lover, is in a state of great depression. A married man, with whom she works, enters into an adulterous relationship with her in order to "comfort her." Fletcher would argue that what he did might very well have been a noble deed, for the man acted out of concern for his friend. What a myopic viewpoint! Let us consider the rest of the story. The man's wife learned of his adulterous adventure, could not cope with the situation, and eventually committed suicide. One of the man's sons, disillusioned by the immorality of his father and the death of his mother, began a life of crime and finally was imprisoned for the murder of three people. Another son became a drunkard and was killed in an auto accident that also claimed the lives of a mother and two children. Now, was that initial act of adultery the "loving" thing to do? Certainly not.

Fourth, situationism assumes that "love" is some sort of ambiguous, no-rule essence that is a cure-all for moral problems. That is like suggesting that two football teams play a game in which there will be no rules except the rule of "fairness." Fairness according to whose judgment? Team A? Team B? The referees? The spectators? That is utter nonsense! Fifth, even when one suggests that "love" be the criterion for ethical decisions, he presupposes some standard for determining what love is. Situationists contradict themselves at every turn.

Determinism

Another false concept regarding human conduct is determinism. Determinism, whether it be social, biological, or theological, has a necessary logical consequence—it absolves man of personal responsibility for his conduct. Let us consider several facts of this general thesis.

Behaviorism, as developed by John Watson (1878-1958), a psychologist at Johns Hopkins University, argued that personality, hence conduct, is the end product of our habit system. Watson taught that man is merely an animal resulting from the evolutionary process. B.F. Skinner of Harvard, who became the leading proponent of behaviorism, believed that man, as an animal, is the product of environment, and so even to speak of human responsibility was nonsense in his view. A practical example of these theories can be seen in Clarence Darrow's defense of murderers Leopold and Loeb, who killed 14-year-old Bobby Franks as an "experiment." Darrow argued that they were in no way responsible for their act since brutal forces of their past had shaped their destinies (see Weinberg, 1957, pp. 16-88).

Sociobiology is a newer notion that attempts to synthesize information from the social sciences with biology. In this paradigm, man is seen as a mere machine, somewhat analogous to a computer, which has been programmed by its genetic makeup. Human behavior is the result of physical and chemical forces, and, as we do not hold a machine accountable, so neither should we man.

A few comments concerning these ideas are in order. First, if determinism is true, there is no such thing as human responsibility. This is a necessary corollary of the theory. In spite of this, determinists frequently speak, write, and act as though human accountability existed. Consistency is a rare jewel among them. Second, if man is not responsible for his actions, such terms as "good" and "evil" are meaningless. Third, if man is not accountable, no one should ever be punished for robbery, rape, child abuse, murder, etc. Do we punish a machine that maims or kills a person? Fourth, how can we be expected to be persuaded by the doctrine of determinism, since the determinists were "programmed" to teach their ideas, and thus these ideas may not be true at all. Fifth, determinists will not abide by their own doctrine. If we recopied Edward Wilson's book, *Sociobiology: The New Synthesis*, and had it published in **our** names, we would find out rather quickly whether Wilson thought we were responsible for the action or if only our genetic backgrounds were!

Is There Ultimate Moral Responsibility?

A crucial question that must be addressed is this: "Is there any ultimate consequence to immorality?" Atheists are fond of saying that one should not be unethical because of social sanctions, i.e., society's disapproval, legal punishment, etc. The implication is, unethical conduct is only "bad" because you might get caught! We once asked an atheist this question: "Paul, the apostle of Christ, and Adolf Hitler are two well-known historical characters. Both are now dead. Now, so far as they are concerned, does it really make any difference that they lived their lives in such divergent directions?" He replied that it did not! If that is the case, human existence makes no sense whatsoever. But that is infidelity's position, of course.

- 71 -

In this chapter, we have discussed human moral obligations. The fact that we have considered morality is something unique to our kind. No two apes ever sat down and said, "Let's talk about ethical obligations today." That ought to say something about our nature. In their book, *Why Believe? God Exists!*, Miethe and Habermas have observed:

> At every turn in the discussion of moral values, the naturalistic position is weighted down with difficulties. It has the appearance of a drowning swimmer trying to keep its head above water. If it concedes something on the one hand, it is condemned on the other. But if it fails to admit the point, it appears to be in even more trouble. It is an understatement to say, at the very least, that naturalism is not even close to being the **best** explanation for the existence of our moral conscience (1993, p. 219, emp. in orig.).

As we draw this discussion to a close, there are some important summary observations that should be mentioned.

1. Human moral responsibility is based upon the fact that God is our Creator (Psalm 100:3), and that we have been made in His spiritual image (Genesis 1:26). Just as a potter has a right over the clay he is fashioning, so our Maker has the right to obligate us morally and spiritually to right living (see Romans 9:21).

2. Since morality is grounded in the unchanging nature of God (Malachi 3:6; I Peter 1:15), it is absolute—not cultural, not relative, not situational.

3. God's will for human behavior is not a matter of subjective speculation that every man figures out for himself; rather, Jehovah has spoken (Hebrews 1:1), and His Mind is made known in objective, biblical revelation (I Corinthians 2:11ff.; II Timothy 3:16-17).

4. Though the Lord possesses an unchanging nature, His revelatory process was progressive

and adapted to man as he spiritually developed in those times of antiquity. Accordingly, in ages of the past Jehovah tolerated, and even regulated, certain acts that are not permissible in the Christian era. This, of course, does not mean that God vacillates in His morality; it simply means that He dealt with man as he was in that infantile state (Matthew 19:8; Acts 14:16; 17:30-31). Today, the New Testament stands as the Lord's final and ultimate standard of morality.

5. Though the New Testament is the "law of Christ" (Romans 8:2; Galatians 6:2), it is not a "legal" system in that each aspect of human conduct is prescribed with a "thou shalt" or "thou shalt not." Yes, there are both positive and negative commands in the New Testament, but they do not spell out every specific activity. The inspired document contains many rich principles that challenge us to develop a greater sense of spiritual maturity and to soar to heights that are God-honoring.

6. One must recognize also that New Testament ethics does not deal merely with actions, but addresses motives as well. For instance, what if one accidentally runs down with his automobile (and thereby kills) a careless pedestrian? He is not held accountable before God, for his act was unintentional. On the other hand, one can be guilty (in disposition) of both adultery and murder (cf. Matthew 5:28 and I John 3.15).

7. It is imperative that men recognize that ethical activity (i.e., right relations with one's fellows) is not the totality of a person's obligation before God. The centurion Cornelius certainly learned this truth (Acts 10). There are spiritual responsibilities that the Lord has pre-

scribed as a test of true faith, and yet men frequently ignore such divine obligations.
8. Finally, even though the Almighty has called His human creation to a high moral level, we must recognize that He is aware that we are but frail, dusty flesh (Psalms 78:39; 103:14). And so His marvelous grace has been revealed in the unspeakably wonderful gift of His Son. Those who in loving faith submit to Him (Hebrews 5:8-9) can know the pardon of their moral blunders (Acts 22:16), and are challenged to live righteous and godly lives in this present world (Titus 2:11-14).

5
CONCLUSION

Theists happily affirm it; skeptics begrudgingly concede it. It is simple logic. **Everything designed has a designer.** Design, at least in part, has to do with the arrangement of individual components within an object so as to accomplish a functional or artistic purpose. An automobile contains design because its many units, engineered and fitted together, result in a machine that facilitates transportation. A beautiful portrait evinces design when paints of various colors are combined, by brush or knife upon canvas, so as to effect an aesthetic response. Rational individuals instinctively recognize the presence of design—for which there are multiplied thousands of examples within the Universe that we inhabit.

Adding to the force of this argument is the principle known as *a fortiori* reasoning. If something is said to follow in an *a fortiori* fashion, it means that the conclusion can be reached with an even greater logical necessity than another conclusion already accepted. Here is an example.

Both a pair of pliers and a computer are tools. If one admits that it took a designer to make the pliers (a conclusion that no rational person would deny), it follows with even greater force that it required a designer to make the computer, since the computer is much more complicated than the pliers. Using *a fortiori* reasoning, it can be established that if the lesser (the pliers) requires a designer, the greater (the computer) **absolutely demands** a designer. Again, this is simple logic.

In making our case for the existence of God, the Grand Designer, we have examined numerous examples of His handiwork throughout the Universe. The design inherent in the Universe itself, and in the living things that it contains, cannot be ignored or explained away. The Universe, plants, animals, and man were not conceived accidentally by "father chance" and birthed by "mother nature."

Yet some would have us believe that is exactly what happened—and they will go to almost any length to avoid the implications of the design in nature that demands a Designer. Why? Atheist Paul Ricci has answered: "...either a divine being exists or he does not; there are no third possibilities regardless of what the skeptic or agnostic says" (1986, p. 140). The tragic fact is that some people are determined not to believe in God, regardless of how powerful, or how overwhelming, the evidence may be. In assessing such an attitude, the psalmist observed: "The fool hath said in his heart, 'There is no God' " (Psalm 14:1). Strong words, those. Yet they were not intended to offend. Rather, they were intended as a commentary on the fact that, indeed, one would have to be foolish to observe the evidence that establishes beyond reasonable doubt the existence of God—and then turn and deny both the evidence and the God documented by the evidence. The Scriptures make it plain that at no time in all of recorded history has God left Himself without a witness of Himself in nature (Acts 14:17). No one will stand before the judgment bar of God in the great day yet to come, shrug their shoulders with indifference, and nonchalantly say with impunity, "I'm sorry I didn't believe in you, but there just wasn't enough evidence to prove you existed." The evidence that establishes the case for the existence of God is simply too plenteous, and too powerful.

REFERENCES

Andrews, E.H. (1978), *From Nothing to Nature* (Welwyn, Hertfordshire, England: Evangelical Press).

Asimov, Isaac (1970), *Smithsonian Institute Journal*, June.

Asimov, Isaac (1975), *Guide to Science* (London: Pelican Books).

Avraham, Regina (1989), *The Circulatory System* (New York: Chelsea House).

Barnett, Lincoln (1959), *The Universe and Dr. Einstein* (New York: Mentor).

Beck, William (1971), *Human Design* (New York: Harcourt, Brace, Jovanovich).

Block, Irvin (1980), "The Worlds Within You," *Science Digest* special edition, pp. 49-53,118, September/October.

Borek, Ernest (1973), *The Sculpture of Life* (New York: Columbia University Press).

Brand, Paul and Phillip Yancey (1980), *Fearfully and Wonderfully Made* (Grand Rapids, MI: Zondervan).

Burnett, Allison L. (1961), *Natural History*, November.

Cahill, George F. (1981), *Science Digest*, 89[3]:105.

Cauwels, Janice (1986), *The Body Shop* (St. Louis, MO: C.V. Mosby).

Cherfas, Jeremy (1984), *New Scientist*, May 17.

Clarke, William N. (1912), *An Outline of Christian Theology* (New York: Charles Scribner's Sons).

Cosgrove, Mark P. (1987), *The Amazing Body Human* (Grand Rapids, MI: Baker).

Darwin, Charles (1859), *The Origin of Species* (London: A.L. Burt).

Darwin, Francis (1889), *Life and Letters of Charles Darwin* (London: Appleton), Vol. I.

Davies, Paul (1992), "The Mind of God," *Omni*, 14[5]:4.

Davis, George (1958), "Scientific Revelations Point to a God," *The Evidence of God in an Expanding Universe*, ed. John C. Monsma (New York: G.P. Putnam's Sons).

Dawkins, Richard (1982), "The Necessity of Darwinism," *New Scientist*, Vol. 94, April 15.

Dawkins, Richard (1986), *The Blind Watchmaker* (New York: W.W. Norton).

DeBakey, Michael E. (1984), in *World Book Encyclopedia* (Chicago, IL: World Book/Childcraft International).

Eccles, John (1958), *Scientific American*, September.

Encycopaedia Britannica (1989), "Bionics," (Chicago: Encyclopaedia Britannica, Inc.).

Estling, Ralph (1994), "The Scalp-Tinglin', Mind-Blowin', Eye-Poppin', Heart-Wrenchin', Stomach-Churnin', Foot-Stumpin', Great Big Doodley Science Show!!!," *Skeptical Inquirer*, 18[4]:428-430.

Estling, Ralph (1995), "Letter to the Editor," *Skeptical Inquirer*, January/February, 19[1]:69-70.

Fletcher, Joseph (1966), *Situation Ethics: The New Morality*, (Philadelphia, PA: Westminster Press).

Frair, Wayne A. and Percival Davis (1983), *A Case for Creation* (Chicago, IL: Moody).

Futuyma, Douglas (1983), *Science on Trial* (New York: Pantheon).

Geisler, Norman L. (1976), *Christian Apologetics* (Grand Rapids, MI: Baker).

Geisler, Norman L. and Winfried Corduan (1988), *Philosophy of Religion* (Grand Rapids, MI: Baker).

Giant Panda Zoobook (undated), (San Diego, CA: San Diego Zoo).

Gore, Rick (1976), *National Geographic*, September.

Gould, Stephen Jay (1980), *The Panda's Thumb* (New York: W.W. Norton).

Gribbin, John (1983), "Earth's Lucky Break," *Science Digest*, 91[5]:36-37,40,102.

Guinness, Alma E., ed. (1987), *ABC's of the Human Body* (Pleasantville, NY: Reader's Digest Association).

Guth, Alan and Paul Steinhardt (1984), "The Inflationary Universe," *Scientific American*, Vol. 250, May.

Guth, Alan (1988), Interview in *Omni*, November, 11[2]:75-76,78-79,94,96-99.

Hawking, Stephen W. (1988), *A Brief History of Time* (New York: Bantam).

Henry, Carl F.H. (1973), *Baker's Dictionary of Christian Ethics* (Grand Rapids, MI: Baker).

Heeren, Fred (1995), *Show Me God* (Wheeling, IL: Searchlight Publications).

Hoyle, Fred (1981a), "Hoyle on Evolution," *Nature*, Vol. 294, November 12.

Hoyle, Fred (1981b), "The Big Bang in Astronomy," *New Scientist*, Vol. 92, November 19.

Hoyle, Fred and Chandra Wickramasinghe (1981), *Evolution from Space* (London: J.M. Dent & Sons).

Humanist Manifestos I and II (1977), (Buffalo, NY: Prometheus Books).

Jackson, Wayne (1993), *The Human Body: Accident or Design?* (Stockton, CA: Courier Publications).

Jastrow, Robert (1977), *Until the Sun Dies* (New York: W.W. Norton).

Jastrow, Robert (1978), *God and the Astronomers* (New York: W.W. Norton).

Jastrow, Robert (1981), *The Enchanted Loom: Mind in the Universe* (New York: Simon and Schuster).

Jastrow, Robert (1982), "A Scientist Caught Between Two Faiths," Interview with Bill Durbin, *Christianity Today*, August 6.

Kautz, Darrel (1988), *The Origin of Living Things* (Milwaukee, WI: privately published by the author).

Lawton, April (1981), "From Here to Infinity," *Science Digest*, 89[1]:98-105, January/February.

Lenihan, John (1974), *Human Engineering* (New York: John Braziller).

Lewontin, Richard (1978), "Adaptation," *Scientific American*, 239[3]:212-218,220,222,228,230.

Macalister, Alexander (1886), "Man Physiologically Considered," *Living Papers*, (Cincinnati, OH: Cranston and Stowe), Vol. VII.

Mader, Sylvia S. (1979), *Inquiry Into Life* (Dubuque, IA: W.C. Brown).

Miethe, Terry L. and Gary R. Habermas (1993), *Why Believe? God Exists!* (Joplin, MO: College Press).

Miller, Benjamin and Goode, Ruth (1960), *Man and His Body* (New York: Simon and Schuster).

Morris, Henry M. (1974), *Scientific Creationism* (San Diego, CA: Creation-Life Publishers).

Morris, Henry M. (1985), *Creation and the Modern Christian* (El Cajon, CA: Master Books).

Murray, I. MacKay (1969), *Human Anatomy Made Simple* (Garden City, NY: Doubleday).

Nourse, Alan E. (1964), *The Body* (New York: Time-Life).

Pfeiffer, John (1961), *The Human Brain* (New York: Harper and Brothers).

Pfeiffer, John (1964), *The Cell* (New York: Time, Inc.).

Pines, Maya (1986), in *The Incredible Machine* (Washington, D.C., National Geographic Society).

Popper, Karl R. and John C. Eccles (1977), *The Self and Its Brain* (New York: Springer International).

Ricci, Paul (1986), *Fundamentals of Critical Thinking* (Lexington, MA: Ginn Press).

Russell, Bertrand (1969), *Autobiography* (New York: Simon & Schuster), Vol. III.

Sagan, Carl (1974), "Life on Earth," *Encyclopaedia Britannica*, Volume 10.

Sagan, Carl (1979), *Broca's Brain* (New York: Random House).

Sartre, Jean Paul, (1961), "Existentialism and Humanism," *French Philosophers from Descartes to Sartre*, ed. Leonard M. Marsak (New York: Meridian).

Sartre, Jean Paul (1966), "Existentialism," Reprinted in *A Casebook on Existentialism*, ed. William V. Spanos (New York: Thomas Y. Crowell Co.).

Scadding, S.R. (1981), *Evolutionary Theory*, May.

Schaller, George B., Hu Jinchu, Pan Wenshi, and Zhu Jing (1985), *The Giant Pandas of Wolong* (Chicago, IL: University of Chicago Press).

Schiefelbein, Susan (1986), in *The Incredible Machine* (Washington, D.C.: National Geographic Society).

Science Digest (1981), January/February, 89[1]:124.

Sedeen, Margaret (1986), in *The Incredible Machine* (Washington, D.C.: National Geographic Society).

Shryock, Harold (1968), "Your Bones Are Alive!," *Signs of the Times*, January.

Simpson, George Gaylord (1949), *The Meaning of Life* (New Haven, CT: Yale University Press).

Simpson, George Gaylord (1951), *The Meaning of Evolution* (New York: Mentor Books).

Sproul, R.C. (1994), *Not A Chance* (Grand Rapids, MI: Baker).

Tait, Katherine (1975), *My Father Bertrand Russell* (New York: Harcourt, Brace, & Jovanovich).

Thaxton, Charles B., Walter L. Bradley, and Roger L. Olsen (1984), *The Mystery of Life's Origin* (New York: Philosophical Library).

Tryon, Edward P. (1984), "What Made the World?," *New Scientist*, Vol. 101, March 8.

Weinberg, Arthur (1957), *Attorney for the Damned* (New York: Simon & Schuster).

White, Robert (1978), *Reader's Digest*, September.

Wylie, Evan M. (1962), *Today's Health*, July.

Wysong, R.L. (1976), *The Creation/Evolution Controversy* (East Lansing, MI: Inquiry Press).

Youmans, W.B. (1979), in *World Book Encyclopedia* (Chicago, IL: World Book/Childcraft International).